Pet Miracles

INSPIRATIONAL TRUE TALES OF OUR BELOVED ANIMAL COMPANIONS

Brad Steiger and Sherry Hansen Steiger

ADAMS MEDIA
Avon, Massachusetts

Published by
Adams Media, an F+W Publications Company
57 Littlefield Street, Avon, MA 02322. U.S.A.
www.adamsmedia.com

ISBN: 1-59337-386-4

Printed in Canada.

J I H G F E D C B A

Library of Congress Cataloging-in-Publication Data
Steiger, Brad.
Pet miracles / Brad Steiger and Sherry Hansen Steiger.
p. cm.
ISBN 1-59337-386-4
1. Pets--United States--Anecdotes. 2. Pet owners--United States-
-Anecdotes. 3. Human-animal relationships--United States-
-Anecdotes. I. Steiger, Sherry Hansen. II. Title
SF416.S76 2005
636.088'7--dc22

2005016013

This publication is designed to provide accurate and authoritative information with regard to the subject matter covered. It is sold with the understanding that the publisher is not engaged in rendering legal, accounting, or other professional advice. If legal advice or other expert assistance is required, the services of a competent professional person should be sought.
　　—From a *Declaration of Principles* jointly adopted by a Committee of the American Bar Association and a Committee of Publishers and Associations

Many of the designations used by manufacturers and sellers to distinguish their products are claimed as trademarks. Where those designations appear in this book and Adams Media was aware of a trademark claim, the designations have been printed with initial capital letters.

While all the events and experiences recounted in this book are true and happened to real people, some of the names, dates, and places have been changed in order to protect the privacy of certain individuals.

Illustration by Stephen Marchesi.

This book is available at quantity discounts for bulk purchases.
For information, call 1-800-872-5627.

Foreword

ACCORDING TO A recent American Veterinary Medical Association survey, 58.3 percent of all American households have at least one pet. There have never been so many pets in America's history as there are now—and they are living longer, healthier lives due to the affection lavished on them by their owners.

Why do we so love to share our homes with pets?

Harvard professor E.O. Wilson, author of *The Diversity of Life*, says that human beings have inherited a tendency to feel an affinity with animals. Throughout the period of about two million years that the human brain evolved to its present form, humans existed in a natural environment and often lived in a symbiotic relationship with animals. Pets help us maintain our link with the natural world, and we are instinctively drawn toward intimate interaction with them.

In the shamanistic traditions of the Native Americans, all creatures are called relatives and considered "people." In the beginning, when humankind was new to the earth, it was the animals who taught us how to survive—and, say the shamans, we still have much to learn from our animal brothers and sisters.

In each of our cultural pasts, whether from Europe, Asia, Africa, or the Americas, our ancestors expressed their kinship with all life by applying the names of animals to their tribal clans. In a way, we still do so today. Consider the names of high school, college, and professional sports teams—all the Tigers, Bears, Bulls, Wolves, and Eagles that challenge one another on a weekly basis in athletic arenas.

Those people who keep pets develop a greater understanding of the sanctity of nature and a reverence for all life, although one person's beloved pet is another's varmint. While nearly everyone can identify with loving a cuddly cat or dog, some people develop a deep and abiding affection for rats or snakes. Creatures that some individuals call pets, others denounce as pests or predators.

In *Pet Miracles*, we'll take you on a kind of literary "Noah's Ark," in which we bring aboard amazing and inspirational tales of men and women who prize their loving relationships with a wide variety of creatures, great and small. We may not have "two of every kind," as did Father Noah, but we will have on board a colorful menagerie of wonderful pet stories.

There is a story that numerous people have shared with us that epitomizes the pet lover's attitude toward animals so very well. As we point out, so many individuals have shared this story with us that it might be a kind of urban legend, but it still carries a wonderful message.

According to the story, a veterinarian has the uncomfortable task of informing a family that their beloved dog is dying of cancer and that the merciful course of action would be to perform euthanasia on their pet. Later, after the dog has made his transition, the veterinarian is talking with the family and sadly wondering out loud why animal lives are shorter than human lives. The family's five-year-old boy speaks up and says that he knows why this is the case.

"Our pastor says that people are born so that they can learn to be good, like loving everybody and being nice to one another," the boy says. "Well, animals already know how to do that, so they don't have to stay as long."

Such an observation "from the mouths of babes" may provide a comforting explanation for many individuals. In *Pet Miracles*, you will read again and again how the selfless, loving actions of animals served, and sometimes saved, their human companions. In less dramatic accounts, you will clearly perceive how the very experience of human-animal interaction can be a miracle in itself.

Sherry Hansen Steiger
Brad Steiger
October 2005

*A*round 1:00 a.m. on Saturday, January 31, 2004, firefighters in Eagan, Minnesota, responded to a smoke alarm at Trinity Lone Oak Lutheran School. When they arrived at the room that had triggered the alarm, they found that the fire had been subdued by Dory, the class fish.

Dory, named after a character in the popular motion picture *Finding Nemo*, is a Beta, a Chinese fish that can breathe air for a limited time and that can flop from one puddle to another. Firefighter Al Taylor spotted Dory on the floor, "looking decidedly unhappy," and called for a glass of water in which to place her.

A Trinity Oak parent told Steve Blumke of the Pioneer Press that it wasn't every day that a fish saved a school, but Dory had saved the day.

According to teacher Linda Krienke, the fire broke out because a candle was left burning in a cardboard box on a desk. The flames spread to workbooks and soon approached the decorated glass vase on the desk that housed Dory. The heat from the fire cracked her bowl and released enough water to squelch the flames. Although the splash of liquid didn't completely extinguish the fire, firefighters said that it managed to stop the fire from spreading to the ceiling. Smoke damage destroyed the classroom computers and numerous other items, but Dory's watery domicile had saved the school from destruction.

Linda Krienke says that Dory, the stalwart survivor, happily swims around in a new bowl.

While even the most enthusiastic champion of Dory is not suggesting that the fish deliberately splashed water out of her bowl to extinguish the flames that threatened the classroom at Trinity Lone Oak Lutheran School, many scientists now maintain that fish do not deserve their long-held reputation as the dimwits of the animal kingdom. On August 31, 2003, the *Sydney Morning Herald* quoted a group of British scientists who said that fish, far from being merely instinct-driven, were manipulative, cunning, and socially aware. Some species of fish have developed strategies of punishment and reconciliation, established cultural traditions, and exhibited impressive long-term memories.

Biologists Calum Brown, Keven Laland, and Jens Krause, writing in the journal Fish and Fisheries, declared that the image of fish as pea-brains should become obsolete. Although it may astonish those individuals accustomed to judging animal intelligence on the basis of brain volume, the scientists wrote, "in some cognitive domains, fishes can even be favorably compared to nonhuman primates."

Results of tests run on fish in aquaria at Oxford University have shown that despite their tiny brains, fish possess cognitive abilities surpassing those of some small animals. On October 3, 2004, Robert Matthews, science correspondent for *The Telegraph* (United Kingdom) summarized the discoveries of Dr. Theresa Burt de Perera (which appeared in the *Proceedings of the Royal Society*) which demonstrate that fish are "very capable of learning and remembering, and possess a range of cognitive skills."

Karen Youngs, the editor of *Practical Fishkeeping*, has commented that she concludes, based on correspondence with the publication's readers, that fish are fully capable of recognizing their owners and, in some instances, may go into a sulk if someone else tries to feed them. Ms. Youngs is not likely to dispute the affection felt for their fish by Pauline and Tom Evans of Bradnich, Devon, England, who claimed in January 2004 that it was quite likely that their family had maintained the longest human-fish relationship in the world. As for the claim that the Evans's fish is the oldest one ever sustained in a bowl, that will have to be tested by marine biologists.

Mrs. Evans's father won three fish at a fair in 1960, and after his death in 1999, Pauline, seventy, inherited the five-inch long sole survivor. Goldie, who was now a bit more silver than gold in color, was still swimming strongly in an 18" by 10" tank after forty-four years.

While it may be supposed that Pauline and Tom Evans genuinely care for Goldie and are fond of the fish, they have yet to give it mouth-to-mouth resuscitation as a sign of their devotion.

On November 4, 2003, Leo van Aert, a fifty-seven-year-old former ambulance driver from Antwerp, Belgium, was celebrating his birthday when he noticed that his beloved koi carp was behaving rather strangely in its fish tank. After making a few jerking motions, the carp became motionless.

Because of his many years as an ambulance driver, Leo immediately perceived that the fish had experienced a heart attack. Without hesitation, he pulled the carp from its tank and gave it heart massage.

After a few minutes of this massaging, Leo told the *Gazet van Antwerp*, his pet began to move so he put it back in the water. It appeared that the carp had responded to the massage and was swimming in its tank as if it were none the worse for wear.

Keeping an alert eye on the fish tank, Leo sat back down to resume the his birthday celebrations. After some minutes of normal activity, the carp again stopped moving.

This time, Leo rushed to the tank, pulled his finned friend from the water, and gave it the "kiss of life." Once he had applied mouth-to-mouth resuscitation, the carp fully recovered and swam happily. Leo had more than his birthday to celebrate that day.

Seventy-year-old Jarrell Willert grew up on a farm in eastern Nebraska, and although the family had a dog, seven or eight cats, three horses, and too many cattle to count, he remembers most the flock of geese that claimed a good share of the apple orchard as their private kingdom the summer when he was eleven.

"Geese are extremely territorial," Jarrell explained to us. "Ada, my eight-year-old sister, and I hated those big gray, long-necked, feathered monsters that would come hissing at us whenever we would happen to violate their unseen boundary lines. There was one gander and about seven females. They had staked out the five apple trees just south of the chicken coop as their sacred land, and if you approached it too close, they would come for you, hissing like a bunch of angry snakes.

"Once you've been grabbed by a goose, you will not soon forget it," Jarrell said. "Their powerful beaks grab hold of you and their mighty wings beat on you until they think you've learned your lesson not to trespass on their territory. Once they let you go, they might peck you hard once or twice to be certain you'll be more careful where you walk in the future."

The only one who could approach the geese was their grandfather, Jake Hamill. (Jarrell had been named for his two grandfathers—Jake Hamill and Darrell Willert: Jarrell.) "Grandpa would walk right up to the big old gander that ruled the flock and scratch his head," Jarrell said. "He called him, 'Sarge.' Grandpa would talk to him just like anyone else would a dog. He'd say, 'How ya doin', Sarge? Keeping an eye on those ladies of yours?' The old gander would lean his head against Grandpa and let him scratch his head and neck. Then Grandpa would take some kernels of corn from his pocket and feed Sarge by hand, never seeming to fear that deadly beak one little bit."

The only time Sarge ever caught Jarrell was when he tried to make friends the way Grandpa Jake did. "I never got within twenty feet of him before he came running at me, flapping his big wings and hissing like some kind of reptilian monster. His beak got hold of the nape of my neck, and his wings pounded my back like a prizefighter gone berserk. I screamed so loud they could've heard me in the next county, and Mom came running and beat Sarge and his harem back with a broom."

The geese made doing farm chores extra difficult for Jarrell and Ada. "When it was time to pick eggs," he explained, "it was so much closer to the hen house if we could cut across the orchard with our wire egg pails. If Sarge and his ladies were there, there was no way they would grant us passage—and we would have to walk the long way around. When we finished feeding the pigs, we might like to treat ourselves to a juicy apple. But there was no such luck if Sarge and his family were home underneath the apple trees. And whenever a fresh batch of goslings were hatched, the new mothers became extra alert to intruders and extra mean to us kids."

There were times when the entire flock would march down to drink at the trough near the cattle tank. "At this point, they would be about twenty yards away from their homestead," Jarrell said. "This was our chance. If we were quiet, we could pick apples or cut across to gather eggs in the henhouse at this time. But if we made too much noise, the ever-alert Sarge would let out a loud honk and the entire goose tribe would come running double-time to secure their kingdom."

Jarrell said that he would never forget the hot July afternoon when their feathered nemesis became their hero.

"It was the summer of 1945," he recalls. "Germany had given up in May and Japan would surrender in August. Luxury items were still very scarce, and some of the necessities were still being rationed, but Dad had managed to buy me a brand new, beautiful red-with-white-stripes bike at Montgomery Ward. I emphasize 'brand new,' because during World War II, it was just impossible for kids to get things like bicycles or anything else with metal and rubber in their composition."

Jarrell was learning to acquire balance and confidence on the gravel lane of their farm. "I had taken some bad spills and really skinned my elbows," he says. "I tried to wipe the scrapes clean with a handkerchief, but I knew I would be picking gravel out of my skin for days."

Little Ada, wanting to help her big brother, would run alongside him as he teetered on the bicycle. Each time he fell, she would help him pick up the bike and dust it off.

"You don't want any scratches on your new bike," she would say solemnly, carefully inspecting the shiny red-and-white finish.

Jarrell had finally accomplished an unsteady, wobbling, fifteen yards or so when their fifteen-year-old neighbor Dwayne came tearing down the lane on his bike and halted just in front of Jarrell.

"I knew that Dwayne was really jealous of my new bike," Jarrell says. "He had gone the duration of the war riding an old rusty bicycle that had probably belonged to his grandmother. I say, grandmother, because besides being old and rusty, it was a girl's bike."

Dwayne laughed at Jarrell on his bike as if it were the single most hilarious sight that he had ever seen. Funnier, even, than a Three Stooges comedy.

"A little squirt like you can't handle a big bike like that," Dwayne decided, once Jarrell stopped laughing. "Let me show you how to ride a bike."

Dwayne jerked the bicycle roughly out of Jarrell's hands and took off down the lane, pedaling furiously, as if he were in a road race. Ada cried, "Dwayne stole your new bike!"

Jarrell assured her that the big teenager was just trying it out and would soon bring it back. "I was really assuring myself more than Ada," Jarrell told us.

After a couple of laps down the lane and back, Dwayne skidded the bike to a halt in front of Jarrell and Ada. As he swung his leg off the bike, he announced that he had decided to trade bikes with Jarrell.

"You can maybe have your bike back in a couple of weeks," Dwayne said, his confident smile turning into a sneer of defiance. "Or maybe I'll keep it for the rest of the summer. I'm leaving you mine so it's all nice and legal like. Just a swap. Any objections?"

Jarrell said that he had plenty of objections. There was no way that he would let Dwayne ride off on his new bike.

"Without another word, Dwayne punched me in the nose," Jarrell recalled. "I remember seeing stars, just like everyone said you would when you got hit. I fell to the ground and the next thing I knew, Dwayne was straddling my chest, holding me down. I was eleven, and he was fifteen, but I fought like crazy until he pinned my arms and told me to give up. He was taking my bike—and that was that. I felt tears swell in my eyes and blood coming from my nose, but he knew that I would try to tackle him if he let me up."

It was then that Dwayne looked around and discovered that the bike was missing. "Ada!" he shouted. "You little snot! Where did you take the bike?"

Ada's voice was almost musical as she called from the apple orchard. "It's right over here, you big bully," she said. "Nyaah, nyaah, nyaah! Come and get it."

Dwayne got off Jarrell and began to run for the apple trees on the edge of the orchard—Sarge's special trees.

"I rolled over and propped myself up on my elbows," Jarrell said. "Ada had managed to roll the bike over to the orchard at a safe time when Sarge and his brood were heading for the water trough. Her taunting shout to Dwayne served the dual purpose of alerting Sarge that someone was trespassing on his private stomping grounds. Dwayne reached the bike about three seconds before Sarge and his harem reached him with their hisses, their wings, and their beaks. Although he had just punched me in the nose and was about to make off with my new bike, I actually felt sorry for him . . . well, maybe not that much."

Dwayne managed to get away from the angry flock of geese and get back on his own bike, peddling as if his backside depended upon it.

"Speaking of Dwayne's backside," Jarrell said, "he took a trip to the woodshed with his father after our dad gave him a call. As for Sarge and his ladies, Ada and I tossed them handfuls of corn every time we met them the rest of that summer. Neither of us ever scratched Sarge's head, though."

On September 22, 2003, fifty-two-year-old Len Richards, a farmer in Morwell, Gippsland, in southeast Australia, was checking his property for damage after a violent storm when a falling tree branch struck him on the head. He was knocked unconscious and suffered serious head injures. Richards's seventeen-year-old daughter Celeste said that if it had not been for the heroic efforts of Lulu, a partially blind kangaroo, her father might have died. Ambulance paramedic Eddie Wright agreed that the farmer might well have died if he had not been found and brought to the hospital in a timely fashion.

In 1993, the Richards family began to care for a female eastern gray kangaroo that was blind in one eye. Because of its infirmity, the authorities allowed the farmers to keep her as a pet. Len Richards and Lulu had bonded very quickly, and she followed him around the farm as he attended to various chores. The whole family loved Lulu, but they acknowledged that the relationship established between the farmer and his pet was very special.

Lulu had been at Richards's side when the branch fell and knocked him unconscious. When he did not get back on his feet, Lulu sensed that her friend was seriously injured and hopped to the farmhouse to alert the rest of the Richards family.

Mrs. Richards and Celeste noticed immediately that Lulu was acting strangely. The kangaroo was always well behaved and quiet, but now she hopped anxiously back and forth in front of the farmhouse and barked loudly. Because Lulu was acting so out of character, the two women concluded that the normally calm kangaroo was definitely trying to get their attention and bring them out of the farmhouse to investigate.

Lulu hopped on ahead, continuing to bark to guide Mrs. Richards and Celeste so that they would walk in the right direction. Finally, they came upon Richards lying unconscious. Lulu, with her chest puffed out, stood guard over her fallen owner until the ambulance arrived.

Dr. Hugh Wirth, president of the Royal Society for the Prevention of Cruelty to Animals, urged the Richards family to nominate Lulu for its National Bravery Award. On April 24, 2004, Lulu was awarded the National Animal Valor Award.

odi Hegwood lives in a rural area outside a small town south of Madison, Wisconsin. When Kibbles, her family's twenty-month-old black Labrador retriever, hadn't come home for dinner at the customary hour of five in the early evening, Jodi wasn't worried. But their rat terrier, Bitzy, became more agitated by the minute when her special friend had not returned.

Although six-year-old Bitzy had not scratched at the kitchen door since she was a pup, she risked a scolding from Jodi and pawed and whined at the door several times. Jodi was deeply aware that Kibbles and Bitzy had a very special connection. Nearly two years earlier,

Bitzy and the Hegwoods' black Labrador, Duchess, had delivered pups at the same time. Since Duchess birthed a whopping seven pups and Bitzy produced three, the Hegwoods decided to take one of the Labrador's "boys" away from her and allow the tiny terrier to be its surrogate mother. Bitzy had immediately taken to the pup and nursed and raised it as her own. The Lab, named Kibbles, made an immediate transfer of its affection, and now, nearly two years later, Bitzy—less than half his size—was still considered his "mama."

About an hour after darkness fell, Jodi became concerned—Kibbles still had not returned. It was the middle of deer-hunting season, and their home was located near hundreds of acres of very dense woods. It was becoming increasingly apparent that Bitzy sensed that something was wrong with the missing Lab. When Porter, Jodi's husband, got home, she urgently explained the situation to him.

"Porter thought we should let Bitzy out of the house to see if she could find Kibbles," Jodi said. "I agreed, and we told Bitzy to go find her boy."

Bitzy hesitated for just a moment, sniffing the air, looking in one direction, then another, as if tuning in her canine radar.

"After a few seconds, Bitzy was convinced that she knew which way to run," Jodi said. "She ran on ahead of us, and it wasn't too long before we heard her piercing howl coming from the darkness. Porter and I ran as fast as we dared through the dark woods, keeping the beams of our flashlights on the narrow deer path ahead of us."

Jodi and Porter ran about fifty yards before they caught up to Bitzy. "When we had her in our flashlight beams, we saw her sitting beside the limp, blood-covered body of Kibbles," Jodi said. "Porter ran to Kibbles and dropped to his knees beside him. 'Oh, my lord,' he shouted, 'Kibbles has been shot! Somehow Bitzy knew it. That's why she was so upset.'"

As Jodi drew closer, she could see a hole in Kibbles' shoulder that was gushing blood. "At first, I thought he was dead," she said. "But when I stood next to him, I could see that his chest was moving slightly. When I called his name, his eyes flickered open, and he whined. He made an effort as if to stand up, then he lapsed back into unconsciousness. All the time, Bitzy kept licking at his wound and crying in pitiful little yelping sounds."

Kibbles' sleek coat of hair was thick with brambles, thorns, leaves, and dirt. It was obvious to Jodi and Porter that he had been shot by a careless deer hunter and that he had struggled bravely, trying desperately to drag himself home.

Gently, Porter picked up the big Lab. "We've got to get Kibbles to the vet. Pronto!"

With Bitzy whining and jumping at his side, Porter began carrying Kibbles toward the house.

Jodi ran back to their place and got into the pickup truck that Porter had parked in the garage when he came home from work. She drove around to the woods behind their house and backed as far as she could until the trail had narrowed to a footpath. Once Porter had carried Kibbles to the cab, Jodi remained at the steering wheel while Porter held the unconscious dog on his lap. Porter wrapped an old sweatshirt around Kibbles's shoulder in an effort to slow the bleeding.

Fortunately for the Hegwoods, the veterinarian in the nearby town was a good friend of theirs, and did not turn them away because it was after hours for the clinic.

"The vet worked for hours to stitch up Kibbles's wound and to stop the bleeding," Jodi said. "He advised us that Kibbles had lost a lot of blood and that we should stay with him that night to keep watch over him. The crisis was not over, by any means."

When the Hegwoods returned home with their badly injured dog, they were startled to discover that Duchess, Kibbles' biological mother, had broken out of her kennel and was nowhere in sight. Then, when they carried Kibbles into the kitchen and placed him on a bed of old blankets and pillows, they discovered that Bitzy was also missing.

"That's when we heard the mournful howling from the woods," Jodi said. "It was really an eerie sound. Porter and I saw that Kibbles was as comfortable as possible, then we went into the woods to find Duchess and Bitzy."

The Hegwoods found the two mothers at the patch of bloody ground where they had discovered Kibbles. Both dogs were howling over the spot where their son had lain injured, struggling to maintain the life force within him.

"Porter ordered them home," Jodi said, "but neither dog obeyed. This was most unusual, for we give all of our dogs lots of love and a positive environment, but we do demand obedience. And generally, we receive it from each and every one of our canine family. But this time, neither Duchess nor Bitzy came at Porter's command. They remained at the patch of bloody grass where their son had lain so badly injured."

Jodi said that she would always remember the reverence in Porter's voice when he put his arm around her shoulder and whispered, "Come on, Honey. Let's go back to the house and see to Kibbles. I think Duchess and Bitzy are praying."

Sometime around three o'clock in the morning, as Jodi and Porter sat vigil over their wounded dog, Kibbles whimpered and propped himself up on his front legs. With another great effort of will and strength, he stood on all four and lapped water from his dish.

Porter knelt beside the Lab, mindful of his injured shoulder, but hugging him nonetheless. "Hey, boy," he said with a sigh of relief, "you're going to make it."

Jodi smiled her agreement from the stove where she had brewing a fresh pot of coffee. Neither of the Hegwoods made any effort to hide their tears of happiness. Their Kibbles had passed the crisis point.

"At that very moment, we noticed that the dogs ceased their mournful howling," Jodi said. "In another couple of minutes, both Duchess and Bitzy were at the back door. Incredibly, they seemed to have sensed that Kibbles' crisis had passed at the exact moment that he had stood up to get a drink." Porter let them in to mill happily around their boy. After a great deal of whining and gentle licking of Kibbles' wounds, Duchess and Bitzy ate and drank for the first time in nearly six hours. When Jodi and Porter went to bed, the two moms were sleeping next to Kibbles, one on either side.

"I firmly believe that some psychic or mystical power that we humans do not fully understand led Bitzy to Kibbles," Jodi said. "I also believe that it was this same power that told the two moms when their son's crisis had passed. Oh, and I also believe that just as Porter said, when Duchess and Bitzy were howling at the spot where we found Kibbles they truly were praying. And we were all thankful that their prayers were answered, for Kibbles fully recovered from that awful wound that nearly claimed his life."

On an autumn evening in 1990, Barbara P. of Thomaston, Connecticut, answered the doorbell of her home and suddenly found herself in frightening situation. With a vulgar curse and a sudden push against the half-open door, a burly drunken man forced his way into her house and demanded to use the telephone.

Barbara staggered back from the man's unwelcome invasion of her home. There was something in his crude and rough manner that warned her he would soon be demanding more of her than the use of her telephone.

Barbara screamed for help. Although on the rational level of consciousness, she was quite aware that there was no one around to hear her cries, it was perhaps sheer reflex or instinct that caused her to shout for help.

It may also have been an instinctive act of love and courage that brought Samantha, Barbara's twelve-ounce African gray parrot, to her rescue. Before the startled invader could defend himself, Samantha had dive-bombed him three times, raking his face with her razor-sharp talons and beak.

At the same time, Gomer, Barbara's fifteen-year-old Chihuahua, roused himself from his nap and joined the fray. His old bones were rather tired and creaky, but no one was going to harm his beloved mistress and get away with it. Besides, Gomer reasoned, it looked as though Samantha could use some help. Without further debate, Gomer sank his tiny teeth into the intruder's leg.

Barbara later told a policewoman who answered her 911 call that once Samantha and Gomer had ganged up on the invader, he began yelling like crazy. Attempting to protect his face from Samantha's aerial attack and doing his best to shake free of Gomer's grinding teeth, the brute ran stumbling and screaming back into the night.

Even before a policewoman had finished with her questions regarding the attack, Barbara made sure to give the courageous Samantha and Gomer an extra-large helping of their favorite treats.

Martin Potter, a bird fancier from Salisbury, Wiltshire, in southern England, bought a cockatiel from a man in Swindon shortly before the winter holidays in 2003. Potter was especially attracted to the cockatiel because its previous owner had taught it to whistle the theme tune from the old Laurel and Hardy comedies. After Potter brought the bird home to his aviary, it wasn't long before the talented whistler had taught the other cockatiels to join in on the tune.

In January 2004, thieves broke into the man's home and, among other items, made off with the four cockatiels. When the detectives interviewed the owner of the birds, he mentioned their penchant for whistling the Laurel and Hardy theme.

The Wiltshire police were at first amused by the cockatiels' fascination with the old tune, but they quickly came to recognize that the birds' quirky trait could also provide a means of their being reclaimed by their owner. The police issued a press release for the media that asked members of the public to listen for any birds whistling the familiar theme.

By mid-February, an anonymous tip came from someone with an ear for music and a memory for Laurel and Hardy films who said that he had heard the distinctive whistle as he traveled through the Bishopdown Farm area of Salisbury. Police followed the tip and later arrested a man and a woman on suspicion of theft. The stolen birds and their cage were returned to Martin Potter.

Shortly after midnight on June 13, 1990, twenty-one-year-old S. Gonzalez broke into a shop that manufactures commercial lighting in Glendale, California. As he made his way cautiously toward the pitch-dark rear of the building, Gonzalez was unaware of two important things that would soon cause him a lot of trouble: 1) The store had an alarm system that picked up noises and relayed them to a security firm, which called the police. 2) Mac, a fifteen-year-old macaw, stood guard.

As he felt his way in the total darkness, Gonzalez approached Mac's perch. That was when the Beaked Crusader decided that the intruder had come far enough.

Out of the shadows came a screeching, scratching, biting fury. Gonzalez screamed in terror, completely unaware of what kind of demon of the darkness had attacked him.

At the same time that the "Big Mac" attack was launched against Gonzalez, the security system recorded the macaw's bloodcurdling squawks and screams, and the police were called.

After a violent thirty-second struggle and a badly bitten thumb, Gonzalez at last managed to get a fist clamped around his assailant's tail feathers—and he dashed Mac to the floor.

The would-be burglar, however, was so confused by the night stalker that had screeched and scratched at him that he stumbled about in a daze, ignoring all the expensive luxury equipment surrounding him. In his bewilderment, he grabbed eleven wrenches and two steering wheels then decided to get out of the madhouse.

Thanks to Mac, the featherweight champion of the lighting company, Gonzalez had been delayed long enough to be caught red-handed by the police as he was leaving the building.

The investigating officers found Mac unconscious on the floor, but the bird recovered nicely from the skirmish.

Steve D., Glendale police detective, said later that Gonzalez had no idea what had hit him. "All he knew was that some sort of monster was tearing at him with bloodcurdling screams. Mac delayed the burglar for a crucial thirty seconds that allowed us to apprehend the suspect. Considering that the suspect is on probation for another burglary charge, Mac performed a great service." The Deputy District Attorney also acknowledged that Mac ". . . had delayed the [burglar] long enough so that police were able to catch him as he came out the front door with tools belonging to the store."

When Paul Richter caught the nice, plump eel in 1970, he envisioned a delicious meal with all the trimmings. However, when he got home, his children refused to let him kill the eel, and they screamed tearfully at the idea of their mother cooking it for their dinner.

Frustrated, confused, and a bit angry, Richter put the eel in one of the family's bathtubs.

Thirty-four years later, the eel is still there. The Richter kids have grown up and left home, but Paul and his wife, Hannelore, of Bochum, Germany, have become so attached to "Eelfie" that he is like one of the family.

In addition to being the recipient of the Richter family's love and affection, Eelfie has become rather famous. In 2003, the Richters appeared on a television talk show with their unusual pet, and in March 2004, Eelfie won an advertising contract to appear in commercials for a German pet food store. In return for his performing on camera, Eelfie will be given a lifetime supply of mosquito larvae, one of his favorite treats.

Marine life experts confirmed the extraordinary relationship enjoyed by the Richters and Eelfie. Generally speaking, eels are best suited for an open water environment and do not do well in a confined space, such as a bathtub. Eelfie, however, has thrived on the red gnat larvae that Paul and Hannelore provide for him.

While the Richters seem content to continue to allow Eelfie to inhabit one of their bathtubs, they may be relieved by their pet's ability to earn some mosquito larvae to lessen the expense of his special diet. According to marine life experts, the oldest eel on record lived for eighty-eight years.

few years ago, when friends would enter Tara Buckland's home in the countryside near Wooster, Ohio, she would greet them with the friendly warning, "Please don't step on my snakes."

One cannot imagine a visitor who would not heed this caution!

Tara had always had peaceful encounters with snakes. In 1989, just after the Chinese New Year ushered in the Year of the Snake, she began to become really conscious of snakes as companions and friends.

A friend of Tara's owned a six-and-half-foot-long red-tailed boa constrictor, who occupied a gigantic glass cage in her living room. When Tara was asked if she wished to touch the snake, she felt no hesitation. She recalled that the large snake was quite heavy and that when the serpent lifted its head to look into Tara's eyes, she felt a "deep jolt, a sense of recognition" that pierced her soul.

After this experience with her friend's snake, Tara began to expend a great deal of time and energy learning all that she could about snakes. She became convinced that snakes were her totem animal and her guides. She acquired several snakes and came to believe that a red Corn snake named Maizey even had healing abilities.

Tara told us that it was by accident that she noticed that Maizey could heal people. A friend was holding the snake when Maizey moved around to her back and fell asleep. Twenty minutes passed, and Tara's friend had to leave so she handed Maizey back to Tara.

"That's when she noticed that her backache had disappeared," Tara explained to us. "After a few more episodes like this, friends began asking if they could hold Maizey."

Maizey never seemed to mind. "She would always crawl on her own to the hurtful spot and then fall asleep or go into trance. When the healing was completed, Maizey would just crawl off the 'patient' and slip down the back of the chair or sofa."

If one wonders just how one goes about communicating with a pet snake, Tara admitted that she was, at first, puzzled by the same question. "Snakes just don't go in much for language," she said. "They don't whine, moan, bark, meow, growl, or yip. Just an occasional hiss."

Tara said that since she loves to talk, it was difficult for her to learn to communicate with silent serpents. She told us that she learned to communicate with non-thought. "Practitioners of Zen recognize this as emptying the mind of conversations and thoughts," she said. "If there is something I wish to communicate, it is best to express the thought, then let it go. When I feel the desire to 'talk' to the snakes, I might use a rattle. Occasionally, I hiss."

Tara told us that in the spring, when snakes come out of winter hibernation, she would throw a "welcome back" party for them. She even had the bakery make a cake with a snake decoration on it. She would invite all her snake-loving friends over to light candles, feast, and sing. The highlight of the evening would be when they would all drum and stamp on the ground to "wake up any sleepyheads."

Recently when we contacted Tara, she told us that her beloved serpent friends have now passed on from old age, and she made the difficult decision not to obtain any more. "It was a fabulous learning experience, and the Snake folks granted me many blessings with them," she said, "but there were also many heartaches, for snake veterinary care is still in its infancy. I still dream about snakes and feel them active in my spiritual growth."

Tara now focuses on providing places for snakes in her garden, and she is active in organizations that work toward habitat preservation. "I have been blessed with some lovely encounters with wild snakes. They have been so patient with me as I fondle and cuddle them before letting them slip back into the forest to live out their days snoozing in tree branches, curled in deep springy moss, or sunning themselves on rocks."

*B*efore British spinster Dolly Duffin died in March 1990, she was frequently seen carrying a hefty turtle named Fred on her shoulder, as one might carry a child. Ms. Duffin was often seen on afternoon walks pushing Fred in a baby carriage.

At the reading of her will, it was revealed that Dolly Duffin had left only a few hundred dollars to a niece, her nearest living human relative, but she had bequeathed approximately $180,000 to Fred, her beloved turtle. According to other terms set forth in her will, Ms. Duffin left her house to the Humane Society with clear instructions that it was to be sold and that all proceeds of the sale should go to the care and keeping of Fred for the rest of his natural life—which could well be another sixty years or more.

There seems no question that Dolly Duffin truly loved her turtle. While others may ask how one could get so attached to a creature that has no soft fur, no sweet song to sing, no back quite large enough to ride, many individuals have enjoyed the unique relationship afforded by a hard shell and a slow, but steady, pace.

We know of a family in Missouri who have been on friendly terms with a turtle since 1921 when Joe, the great-grandfather, found her on his farm and christened her Tessa. There was just something about the turtle that appealed to Joe. Since turtles look pretty much alike, he wanted to be able to recognize Tessa whenever they happened to come across one another. He knew that the blade of his pocketknife wouldn't pierce Tessa's hard shell or hurt her, so he carefully carved the year and his initials on her back.

Ten years later, Rudolph, Joe's son, happened upon Tessa and found his father's initials engraved on her back. Bemused, he added his own initials on the turtle's hard shell.

In 1936, Rudolph's son Floyd and his cousin Dave made the acquaintance of the turtle. Old Tessa had become an integral element in the family folklore, so Floyd and Dave just had to take out their pocketknives and engrave their initials on her shell.

After that, no member of the Missouri farm family came across Tessa in creek or pasture for over fifty years. Although Tessa was kept alive in memory around the dinner table at family gatherings, it was assumed that their unique pet had passed away.

Then, one day in 1988, Floyd's son Don happened upon Tessa going peacefully and methodically about her own turtle business. Don was certain that the turtle was the original Tessa, for there on her shell were the initials that his great-grandfather, grandfather, father, and cousin had carved on her shell.

We last heard about Tessa in 1991 when sixty-six-year-old Floyd found her again. In June of that year, Floyd, with a bit of ceremony, carved the initials of Don's newborn son on the shell of the amiable old turtle. For seventy years, their unique pet has carried the family history on her back.

"Bonding with a pet is a rite of passage that often creates lasting memories for those fortunate enough to experience it," observed our friend, Jolen Marya Gedridge, who lives in a suburb of Detroit. Jolen's many bonding experiences with pets have been varied, but none quite matched her family's experiences with Felix, a South American side-necked turtle.

Jolen tells it in her own words:

"Felix joined our menagerie when I was around two years old. When he came from the pet store, he was slightly smaller than a silver dollar, but he grew up and into an integral part of our family by showing an amazing talent for 'breaking out of his shell' to make a place for himself in our hearts.

"Mostly because of my mother's loving care, Felix is now the size of a dinner plate. Her doting attention to Felix, as well as many other critters, has earned Mom the nickname 'Mother Nature.' When Felix grew a tumor on the side of his neck, she sought out a herpetologist to remove it. Only 'Mother Nature' would spend $400 to save a fifty-cent turtle! Like any good mother, there is no sacrifice too great to keep her family in the best of health and that includes the amphibian relatives. Mom loves and nurtures Felix like any of her children, and he has bonded to her as if he were indeed one of her offspring.

"Through the years, Felix has learned to track Mom down like a trained bloodhound on a search and rescue mission. He puts his nose to the ground, and with a mighty sniff he's off and running in her direction. If Mom's not nearby, Felix will plod through the house until he finds her. In the bathroom? Nope. Computer room? Uh-uh. He continues his quest for turtle TLC! Once he spots her, he takes off, (okay, he lumbers!), in her direction. If she doesn't see him, he announces his presence by nibbling her on the ankle or tugging on her sock or pant leg, letting her know he needs some attention. Once she finishes her chores, she'll scoop him up for a spot of sun under his favorite lamp and some scrumptious turtle treats.

"What kind of a treats tickle a turtle? Obviously a turtle with discriminating taste, Felix will only eat Boston bib lettuce, turning up his shell at garden-variety iceberg or romaine. And, like a truly refined reptile, he prefers his bib in the evenings, when he can dine in seclusion as if he were munching water lilies and plant growth in his native habitat. Cheerios, pumpernickel bread, canned dog food (beef, of course!), and other human goodies round out the 'spice' of Felix's dietary life. After a snack and a spot of sunbathing, Felix goes on the prowl once more, this time after Dad.

"Over the years, Dad has become something of a nemesis to Felix. Mostly because he never gives Felix the attention he wants and always pushing him away. Now that Felix is a 'big boy,' he prefers to engage the old man by challenging him to a fight! Felix tries to show Dad who's boss by cocking his shell toward the edge of the recliner and wedging it underneath: an attempt to flip Dad over on his back—the ultimate in turtle humiliation! Of course, it never works, but at least he shows Dad there is a price to pay for his indifference! After repeated attempts, Dad finally loses his patience and bellows for Mom to remove her terrarium terrorist from his midst. Mom dutifully returns Felix to the safety of his watery lair. After a long, hot soak, he'll grab the sides of his spa and pull himself out, landing with a thud on the tile floor. The sound of shell meeting ceramic tile serves as an early warning system announcing Felix's return to the hunt. His next conquest? ME!

"Felix has always come after me in the bathroom, taking advantage of a stationary target as I stood in front of the mirror trying to do my hair. Felix goes into a figure-eight flight pattern, nipping at my toes and jeans as he passes. If I try to move or do the "Don't Bite Me" dance, he takes up the challenge, chasing me to the best of his toddling ability. As I do my dance, I aim my big toe into the webbing of his feet. A direct, loving touch sets him to increased attacks on my lower appendages. As I leave the bathroom kill zone and head to the living room, Felix follows me like a very slow puppy.

"As I sit in the living room, he'll bank the corning full-throttle toward me. As he nears, I lift my feet about eight to twelve inches off the ground, forcing him to stretch his long neck to grasp my sock. I let him win the tug of war, and Felix proudly claims his newfound booty, stashing it under the coffee table. Victory at last! Once in a while, Felix adds one of my leather sandals to his horde of swag under the coffee table. I figure he enjoys the thrill of the hunt. This kept him active mentally and physically, and it kept me entertained as well.

"Another entertaining pastime in Mom's house is the game of 'Find Felix.' The family plays this game after Felix disappears from sight. Sometimes we find him under Dad's recliner, sometimes under the couch or coffee table. We've also found him in the computer room or kitchen, nose to the ground, adding to his extensive scent map of the house by boldly sniffing where no reptile has sniffed before.

"During the winter, Felix and his 'scintillating' sniffer go into semihibernation mode; responding to the season by snoozing under his lamp for days and sometimes weeks without food or drink. If the urge to submerge strikes him while on walkabout in the house, Felix will crawl under a towel or rug in the bathroom and snooze away the week. When he wakes to find himself hungry or needing to return to his turtle pond, Felix will seek out Mom for nourishment, often trailing his towel behind him in costume as the lesser-known superhero 'The Caped Crusader.' Mom returns Felix to his haven, tucking him in with a leaf of Boston Bib to tide him over lest the midnight munchies strike while the humans sleep.

"While the bib lettuce may satisfy his nutritional pangs, Felix often needs to ease the pangs of isolation as well. As a result, he often makes a midnight escape in search of the human companionship to which he has grown so accustomed. Proving 'no shell is an island,' Felix will make his way to Mom's bedroom; only to be discovered in the morning sleeping soundly under her side of the bed, nestled at the top corner directly below her pillow! Upon discovering her unannounced visitor, Mom gathers Felix close to her body, lovingly clearing the dust bunnies from his webbed feet as she returns him to his sanctuary for treats, sunbathing, and another day of inter-species love that has become the norm in my family's life."

Jolen and her family know that their interactions with this intelligent, playful creature are unique. Truly, Felix has become a member of the family.

When attractive, twenty-four-year-old Thea Atney is out walking Umi and Victor, muggers, mashers, and molesters had better give them a wide berth. Victor is a burly German shepherd, and Umi is a Vietnamese pot-bellied porker that devoutly cherishes the belief that he is a vicious watch hog.

"The dog barks and the pig bites," Thea says, giving fair warning. It immediately becomes very clear that, together, the two make a perfect pair of four-legged bodyguards.

The house-trained porker could easily tip the scales at 150 pounds when he achieves his full-grown dimensions.

Thea acquired the pig just a few months before she got the German shepherd, and she raised the two together.

Dog and hog patrol Thea's home in a village near London, England, and keep wary eyes and keen nostrils on the alert for intruders. Her boyfriend feels much more at ease when he is away, just knowing that Umi and Victor are standing sentry duty.

Thea admitted to us that Umi has snapped his snout at a deliveryman and has chased away dozens of uninvited salesmen. She advised that if the pig takes a liking to a stranger, he will wag his skinny little tail, just like Victor. Should he not be favorably impressed with a stranger, she warns, Umi snorts, lowers his head, and charges.

'He truly is a force to be reckoned with,' she said.

In September 1991, California psychologist Sherry Lebeck revealed that she was employing two potbellied pigs named Louie Louie and Sooey-Heart to cheer patients in her visits to senior centers, hospitals, and schools.

Ms. Lebeck stated that her two "assistant therapists" were especially effective in lifting the spirits of Alzheimer's patients.

In numerous instances, the psychologist said, patients who would not communicate with human therapists and counselors readily responded to Louie Louie and Sooey-Heart. Sooey-Heart is a special favorite because he allows people to touch him, flopping over on his side when his belly is rubbed.

Ms. Lebeck observed that many of her patients came from rural backgrounds. "So when they see a pig, we see an immediate reaction. The patients' long-term memories kick in, and they'll start telling stories about the pigs they remember from their childhood."

On May 19, 2004, Bernd Mottl, Director of the Moenchengladbach opera house in West Germany, announced that he had selected a pot-bellied pig named Berta to star in the new production of Friedrich von Flotows' opera *Martha*. Six pigs had tried out for the part, but most of them appeared too nervous during the audition to be able to withstand the rigors of starring in an opera. A veterinarian approved of the choice of Berta over Niklas and Emma, the final two candidates for the coveted role. He explained that pot-bellied pigs are more stress-resistant than ordinary farm pigs.

Director Mottl informed Berta's owners that they could assist their pig's ascent to stardom by allowing to practice at night by listening to some of Flotows' music on the stereo. When the Westdeutsche Zeitung questioned Directort Mottl regarding Berta's role in the opera, he explained that her main job would be to stand around and simply be a pig.

*I*n January 1991, fifty-two-year-old truck driver Johnny White, his wife Donna, and their French poodle Sabre were making good time on a Pennsylvania highway headed for Buffalo, New York. Johnny was always pleased when Donna and Sabre kept him company on the long hauls from his home base in Texas. They would sing along to the tapes of favorite music that Johnny would always bring with him, and sometimes even Sabre would join in on the high notes. The cab of the big truck would be warm with song, love, and good cheer on even the coldest of winter days.

This wonderful life came to an abrupt end on this particular day when the rig skidded on a patch of ice and slid over a cliff. Johnny was aware that the three of them were tossed about in the truck's cab as the vehicle crashed toward the bottom of a ravine. When he regained consciousness in an emergency room, Johnny was told that he had suffered severe injuries in the accident. A few minutes later, in answer to his desperate query about his wife's condition, he was given the tragic news that his beloved Donna had been killed instantly.

Johnny was flown to a care center in Brownwood, Texas, his hometown. He was so grief-stricken over the loss of his wife that it was some time before his thoughts focused on the plight of Sabre. What had happened to the little dog that both he and Donna had loved so much?

As he lay in the hospital bed recovering from his near-fatal injuries, Johnny grew increasingly depressed. There seemed little possibility that Sabre had survived the awful accident. And even if she had, where was she now? Surely, if she had managed to emerge alive from the crash, some compassionate ambulance or rescue worker would have taken her to be with him at the hospital. No, he told himself blinking back tears, Sabre, too, was dead. He had lost both his beloved wife and their dear little dog.

One day, nearly three months after the accident, a sympathetic dispatcher at Johnny's trucking company's home office in Springdale, Arkansas, decided that he would try to learn what really happened to Sabre. The dispatcher knew that Johnny was bereaved and tormented with doubts about the actual fate of his tiny French poodle. Reasoning that he had nothing to lose but a few minutes' time, the dispatcher got on the radio and put out an urgent appeal on the truckers' network to see what could be learned about Sabre's fate.

Within a few hours a trucker who had come upon the accident scene that January night called in. He remembered seeing a little French poodle cowering and whimpering in a corner of the truck's bed. The trucker was certain that he saw one of the rescue workers take the dog.

It didn't take long to track down the rescue workers who had responded to the accident. Given the death of the woman in the cab and the serious injuries of the driver, they thought they were doing the right thing when they took the French poodle to a local animal shelter.

A telephone call to the animal shelter soon revealed that the little dog hadn't been there very long before she had been adopted by an elderly couple and taken to their home.

When the dispatcher made Johnny's sorrow and tragic circumstances known to Sabre's foster owners, they quickly surrendered the poodle to a trucker heading south toward Tennessee. From there, she was handed over to a driver bound for Little Rock, Arkansas. In

Little Rock, Sabre changed rigs again, this time to a truck with the destination of Springdale. Once there, the French poodle was taken to the home of one of Johnny's closet friends. At last, it was left for Johnny's brother to carry Sabre on the last leg of the odyssey from Springdale to Brownwood. Members of the truckers' network had transported the French poodle a total of 1,700 miles to reunite her with her owner.

Johnny will always cherish the memory of the moment that Sabre first set eyes on him again. She bounded all over the room, turning flips, and racing in circles around his legs, yipping and barking. Finally, she jumped into his arms.

After three terrible months of separation, an awful time of uncertainty and sorrow, Johnny and Sabre were back together again. And after a few more weeks of recuperation on Johnny's part, the two of them were back on the road.

Before they left on their first trip without Donna, they stopped at the cemetery and placed fresh flowers on her grave.

*T*exas sheepherders and goat ranchers raise nearly 4 million sheep and Angora goats annually, but federal environmental restrictions on traps and poisons created a big problem with marauding coyotes. As the coyote population grew in ever-larger numbers, herd losses moved up the scale with them. Texas sheepherders began to lose upward of $9 million in livestock each year.

The classic well-trained sheep dogs cost a lot of money to purchase and a great deal of time to train. And, once a trained dog is performing efficiently, it quite naturally has to be fed regularly or the sheep are going to start looking very tasty to its hungry eyes.

The answer to the ranchers' problem finally revealed itself in the humble figure of the braying donkey.

Once a donkey has established its territory, it becomes extremely possessive of its turf. Donkeys have a natural disliking for coyotes, wolves, and dogs, and they will immediately attack any prowling coyote with hooves and teeth, driving the predator away or even killing it.

As one rancher put it, "All you have to do is to drop a donkey off near your herd and forget about it. It will make friends with the sheep or goats, establish its territory, and protect the critters against predators around the clock. And you don't need to bring food out to the donkey two or three times a day. It will forage for itself on the grasses growing in the area—donkeys are vegetarians."

Another rancher emphasized the often-ignored fact that donkeys are highly intelligent. "Folklore and fables have made the poor donkey the butt of so many jokes that make the animal out to be stupid. It just isn't so. And the donkey also has a great level of endurance and hardly ever gets sick."

An official with the Texas Agriculture Department stated that the donkey has filled an important need in helping ranchers protect their stock. According to recent estimates, more than 1,800 Texas sheep and goat ranchers have now turned to guard donkeys, which can cost as little as $150 each.

When sheepherders in Alberta, Canada, began to complain of increased losses due to coyote attacks on their flocks, the province's department of agriculture suggested that they use guard donkeys as their protectors.

Although highly skeptical at first, a rancher near Vermillion, in Alberta, who had been bedeviled by coyotes raiding his livestock pens, said that he had no problems after his guard donkey arrived.

Another rancher who lost twenty-six goats and six lambs in two months to the wily coyotes admitted that he hired a guard donkey only as a last resort. "We had been terrorized by packs of coyotes for eight years," he said. "But from the day that we got our guard donkey, we have not lost a single animal to predators."

One rancher commented about the friendship that develops between a guard donkey and his fleecy buddies, "The sheep seem to accept the donkey as a member of the flock."

It would have been expected if the petite, pixie-like child standing before us had been too bashful to tell us the story her mother, Beverly, volunteered on her behalf for our Pet Miracles book. We half thought she was about to run off down the aisle or take a timid slide behind her mother and the shopping cart in front of her. Carrie Forester had been browsing the toy section in a department store—quite contentedly, we should add—when she was suddenly retrieved. We were introduced as the authors to whom she should tell her pet story.

Trying our best to not force the issue, it surprised us when from the mouth of this adorable but bashful looking child came an immediate response: "Oh, yes, Alvin is the best pet there ever was." Cassie announced this with her eyes beaming, beseeching us to ask her more.

With an expression of surprise on her face, and before Cassie could continue, Beverly felt compelled to explain that Alvin is a hamster and was a gift for Cassie on her sixth birthday. In a near whisper, Beverly added they had been through a year and a half of trauma, and this was the first time she heard her daughter speak quite that boldly and eagerly to strangers—especially with such a glowing look on her face.

"You see, Cassie had expectations of something larger—like a dog—and I'm so happy to hear her say she could never have a better pet! She and I had many go rounds, if you know what I mean," Beverly winked. "There were many buckets of tears shed along with quite a few bouts of pouting and sulking when I stood my ground that it wasn't the right timing for a puppy."

Undaunted, Cassie waited patiently as her mother recounted the unfortunate set of circumstances that led to a divorce, necessitating the sale and move from their beautiful home into a fourth-floor apartment building.

"We promised Cassie that she could have a puppy when she turned five years old," Beverly said, "but I simply couldn't handle the responsibility and training of a puppy after my divorce, so I went through the whole 'but you promised me' thing, and guess who was the culprit and the mean one? Cassie seemed to blame me for everything and the promised, but not delivered puppy—became a psychological blackmail between mother and daughter and, I suppose, a target of her confusion, anxiety, and grief."

Beverly told us that it took Cassie many months even to act as if she liked the sandy-colored hamster that had been presented to her in a huge wrapped package topped with a gigantic bow in a grand manner at her fifth birthday party. After ripping the colorful birthday paper off in hopes she would see a puppy in the cage, not a little "mousie hamster," Cassie had run back into her bedroom and slammed the door. Beverly said that she did her best to downplay the incident and then waited a few days before placing the oversized cage, replete with a special exercise wheel, water bottle, and hamster toys in Cassie's room.

At this point in the story, Cassie looked right up at her mother and moved in close to give her a hug. "Maybe it really is true that sometimes the best things come in small packages, Mommie, because now I wouldn't even trade Alvin for a puppy!"

With that proclamation, Cassie told us about her friend Alvin.

Cassie admitted she did not think she was going to like her hamster even a little bit. It took several months to give the hamster a name—and that occurred spontaneously after hearing a song on the radio several weeks before Christmas. "Alvin" was one of the singing Chipmunks, and the song had sparked the perfect name for the little pet that she had simply been calling "rat."

Cassie had warmed up to Alvin after he was blessed with a name. When Beverly took a pile of clean clothes into Cassies's room or happened to be walking by—she'd hear Cassie talking to someone else. This often caught her by surprise because she didn't think there was anyone else in the room, but it sounded like Cassie was talking to a playmate. Cassie would often rush into her room after school, taking Alvin out of his cage to let him cuddle up to her while she watched a favorite television program. Cassie commandeered some of her Barbie and Ken clothes, dishes, and furnishings, dressing up the cage and Alvin. Cassie generally obeyed the rules of not letting Alvin be outside the cage unless she watched him carefully and did not let him wander more than several feet from her. She'd even devised a little hamster leash that Alvin gradually seemed at ease with—except on one occasion.

On Valentine's Day, Alvin didn't take to being on this little leash, and Cassie felt sorry for him, freeing him "for just a few minutes" while she was talking on the phone with her friend Jan before she was to leave for school. She was asking her friend how many cookies to bring, just to be sure she remembered right. Beverly was in the kitchen, putting the final touch of frosting and decorations on the Valentine cookies that she and Cassie baked the day as a gift to her first-grade class when there was a knock on the door. The mailman greeted Beverly with a smile, holding up an oversized package with just a few cents of postage due.

Later that day—following school and work—mother and daughter arrived back home, laughing about what a great day they'd had, and how it had ended with their fun dinner with friends. Cassie was still chattering about how much the kids in her class loved the cookies as she walked in her room to get Alvin—the hamster was nowhere to be seen. In all the commotion and excitement of the morning, no one realized that little Alvin snuck out the door of the apartment!

Frantically screaming and crying, and blaming her mom, Cassie searched everywhere—in corners, under furniture, under the beds—to no avail. For days mother and daughter searched, knocked on doors, put up flyers in the hallways and called friends. Beverly hadn't seen the despondent side of her daughter for quite some time, and its reappearance took her off guard.

"I couldn't seem to console Cassie, and that old bitterness came back with the anger and blaming attitude that it was somehow my fault, when a miracle happened," Beverly told us. "Cassie had been praying out loud that God help her bring her best friend back. I couldn't believe my eyes as I opened the front door to check a scratching noise I heard outside our apartment. In comes Alvin, like he'd been on a scouting mission and was suddenly struck homesick. That little hamster walked straight into Cassie's room, like he knew exactly where he was headed, climbed up the bed, and nuzzled himself into the nape of her neck and hair—while she lay there crying! I've never seen anything like it!"

The Foresters heard from neighbors around the apartment building that Alvin had been spotted in the laundry room in the basement. Nobody could catch him, and rumor was that some renters thought he was a mouse and called management. Others said Alvin had been sighted out in the street near the apartment building. They had recognized him from the posted "missing" signs around the neighborhood.

"That little hamster had become my daughter's comforter, friend, cuddle mate, and companion during a time of crisis when she felt her world was upside down," Beverly told us. "Who would ever think that the love of that little critter could turn a little girl's heart around? I couldn't bear it when Alvin was gone. He was so tiny and vulnerable. How could he have made it all the way down five flights of stairs and still find his way back home, unscathed? Maybe Alvin was meant to be in Cassie's life. To hear her say she would never trade him for anything—even a puppy—is a double miracle."

Cassie smiled, and joined in the sentiment: "That's right, Mommy, not even for a puppy!"

*I*t wasn't because the Petersons didn't love Trixie that they decided she should be put to sleep. It was just that the poor little dachshund had an incurable skin disease that the veterinarian called allergic dermatitis, which caused endless itching and a discoloration of the skin.

The medical bills were becoming a terrible drain on the limited resources of Roberta and Claude Peterson of Baton Rouge, Louisiana—usually totaling $75 a month. And then there was the expensive special food for Trixie.

And since Claude, at age seventy-eight, had diabetes, and both he and Roberta had heart problems, they no longer had the physical energy to properly take care of Trixie.

But when the seventy-one-year-old Roberta took Trixie to the veterinarian, Dr. Al Haase talked her out of putting the eight-year-old dachshund to sleep.

Feeling somewhat guilty that they had even entertained such a thought, Roberta agreed with the vet that Trixie shouldn't be eliminated because of circumstances that were no fault of her own.

It was only a few months later when Trixie repaid in full her debt of continued life. Claude suffered a severe insulin reaction and fainted in the bathroom. As he fell into the bathtub, he cut his arm deeply enough so that he could have bled to death if left unattended for very long.

Trixie, however, was on the alert. She ran into the room where Roberta was watching television, jumped up on her lap, barked at her, then jumped off and began tugging at her bathrobe, pulling her toward the bathroom. Opening the door, Roberta was stunned to discover her husband slumped over the tub, bleeding profusely from his arm.

By the time Claude reached the hospital, he was in a coma. It took five hours for the medical staff to get his blood sugar level back to normal so that they could feel right about releasing him.

Roberta and Claude said that they owed Trixie their heartfelt thanks for the opportunity of celebrating their fifty-second wedding anniversary.

Dr. Haase nominated Trixie for the Louisiana Veterinary Medical Association's 1992 "Pet of the Year" award, and the committee agreed with his recommendation. The Baton Rouge veterinarian told writer Chanda Peterkin that Trixie was a real hero, deserving of the award. "People can learn from her story that animals are special and courageous creatures."

he late University of Toronto author and lecturer Ian Currie shared with us a remarkable instance of psychic bonding that occurred between an elderly West Virginia coal miner and a rat that inhabited the dark tunnel.

"The old man, who owned a small mine and worked it himself, noticed that one particular rat would stay near him, as if keeping him company, while he worked at the coal face," Currie said. "Over a period of several months, the two became accustomed to one another.

"The miner would feed the rat from his lunch box, and when it came time to fire the shots that would bring down the coal face, he would chase the rat away so it would not be injured.

"One day, while the miner was working alone," Currie continued the account, "the rat appeared to be unduly agitated and kept scampering up to the miner, then running off. Intrigued, the man put down his drill and followed the rat around the corner to see if he could figure out what was bothering the creature. He had just moved away from the face when the roof collapsed in the exact spot where he had been working."

The miner, according to Currie, would certainly have been killed without the rat's warning. "But how the rat knew the roof was about to collapse and why he warned the man is presently one of the mysteries of animal-human interaction. Currie added, "I think that the rat employed an animal's intuition for danger, and somehow it was able to communicate with the human who had befriended him."

P.M.H. Atwater, L.H.D., Ph.D., is one of the original researchers in the field of near-death studies, having begun her work in 1978. Today, her first two books, *Coming Back to Life* and *Beyond the Light*, are considered the "Bibles" of near-death experience studies. She is also the author of several other books, including *Future Memory* and *We Live Forever: The Real Truth about Death*.

Dr. Atwater has lectured twice at the United Nations and at many other gatherings large and small in the United States, Canada, Europe, and South Korea. She has appeared on countless radio shows and has been a guest on such TV talkshows as *Larry King Live*, *Live with Regis & Kathy Lee*, and *Geraldo*.

Now a resident of Charlottesville, Virginia, Dr. Atwater has been a dear friend for over thirty years. We were delighted when she shared this story about her family's experience with a most unusual rat. As Dr. Atwater tells it:

"It was the last day of school before summer vacation. The sixth grade teacher busily assisted each student in cleaning out desks, lockers, and storage areas and asked for volunteers so that all classroom pets could be adopted. My youngest daughter Paulie happily raised her hand.

"That's how it happened. Without my permission or knowledge or any form of advance preparation, a most unusual rat named DeeDee accompanied my daughter home from school.

"DeeDee was a hooded rat (white body, black head and chest). She was mature, although she had yet to produce a litter. She came complete with cage and water tube wired to one side, straw, and a few food pellets. The older children were horrified to see her; my husband puzzled, and I tried to be reasonable. Paulie begged and begged, promising to take full responsibility for the rat's care and feeding. In that moment of weakness all parents are guilty of, DeeDee was allowed to stay. The spot where her cage sat came to alternate between both kitchen and utility room.

"I noticed right away her special habits. After eating, that rat would tap her water tube with the upright palm of a forepaw, exactly the way a human would use a hand, then she would cup both forepaws to receive the water her tapping had released. She splashed that 'handful' of water over her face and mouth and tapped some more, for enough water so that she could clean out each ear with an extended finger.

"I shook my head in disbelief the first time. But it wasn't long before I found myself studying her, especially when she seemed preoccupied with something else.

"No doubt about it. DeeDee was an educated rat. Maybe it was the sixth-grade classroom she had 'graduated' from. I don't honestly know. All I know is, that rat was more human than animal. You could think her name in your mind, and she would perk up immediately and look at you. You could verbally converse with her, and she would cock her head and listen. If you gave her a command, she would obey it. Change the words you used and she might have to think about her response, but she'd still respond—correctly.

"She knew the difference between up and down, left and right, in and out; and she knew the name of each member of our family." Paulie said DeeDee had free run of the eraser tray under the blackboards along two walls of the classroom. "Although DeeDee had behaved as a regular rat at school (except for her forays along the eraser tray), once in our home, she acted as if she had been trained by a professional animal trainer—in fact, better.

"And you could converse with her. I mean you could carry on a fairly intelligent conversation, and the rat would respond appropriately . . . as if she understood every word.

"Naturally, it didn't take much time before all family members noticed DeeDee's unique temperament and her unusual intelligence. She became more than a pet. She became 'family.'

"If one of us became ill, she would mope around and feign illness herself until that individual recovered. How she could pick up on such timing, I could never tell. She seemed to automatically 'take on' anyone else's condition. After being bred several times and raising equally intelligent babies (she taught them all she knew), DeeDee became seriously ill, and we put her to sleep so she would not suffer.

"With DeeDee gone, Paulie marched up to me one day and announced that DeeDee would come back. 'Just wait and see,' she said.

"Several decades later, after my youngest daughter and I had moved from Idaho to the state of Virginia, and Paulie had given birth to her first child, she chanced upon a most unusual rat while absentmindedly wandering through a shopping mall pet store. She bought the rat and brought it home with her. Her infant son immediately pointed to the rat and attempted to say the name 'DeeDee.'

"Paulie spun around and looked again, then called out, 'DeeDee?'

"The rat jumped up and down, ran round and round, tapped her water tube, cupped her hands, splashed water over her face, and with long slender 'fingers,' cleaned out her ears. After such frenetic activity, the rat sat on her haunches, moved her nose closer to her cage wires, and Paulie swears . . . she smiled at her.

"Paulie named her DeeDee II.

"I went to visit one day. Nothing was said to me about my grandson's new pet. I spied the rat in her cage, and walked over for a closer look. The female was gray-hooded, instead of black as DeeDee had been, so I thought nothing of it and turned to leave—when the rat started banging her cage and jumping up and down.

"I bent over and studied her. She reached out a paw to touch me. When our 'fingers' met, a chill coursed through me. DeeDee! No doubt about it. The family's new pet was DeeDee come back.

"Paulie grinned and the baby giggled.

"I didn't know that animals could reincarnate—and with their same owners. DeeDee's return must have taken some doing, for we now live on the opposite side of the country from where we used to and my youngest daughter has become an adult. Yet Paulie's baby knew the rat, and the rat knew that the baby was Paulie's!

"I have no idea how this happened. I only know DeeDee, the educated rat, had come back, and she was just as clever and just as intelligent as ever.

"It is true, at least as nearly as anyone can tell, that an animal can individualize once it shares life with a human—that is the 'gift' we give our pets. But the extent to which an animal can be and evolve is still hotly debated, even in esoteric circles. As a researcher of the near-death experience and spiritual transformation, I can say this: Animal pets are often there to greet those who cross over in death. The companionship we form with them is lasting."

*E*leven-year-old Alfredo Iannone of Salerno, Italy, no doubt knew very well that he and his friend should not be climbing around on the roof of a building under construction. That thought probably acquired a whole new dimension of truth when he walked too close to the edge and tripped.

As he plummeted through space, Alfredo remembered screaming and thinking that he would surely die.

If not death, then surely terrible injury would have been his fate from having fallen thirty-five feet if it had not been for Stella, his big, part–German shepherd, who made a selfless dash to position herself directly under her master's falling body.

Later, Alfredo recalled that it had been 'falling onto a mattress.' In front of startled eyewitnesses, the boy bounced off the back of the stalwart Stella and onto the ground. Except for a few bruises, he was completely unharmed. Stella, too, was none the worse for wear for having served as living safety net for her careless master.

Alfredo's friend said that Stella had been barking at them from below, as if she were warning them to be careful and scolding them for being so foolhardy. Stella had 'run like a bullet' to position herself under Alfredo.

A physician at the Salerno Public Hospital was yet another voice of praise, declaring Stella a hero. In his opinion, Alfredo would have been killed if the big dog had not raced under him to cushion his fall.

Four-year-old Livia Ungureanu had no doubt been scolded many times for throwing food to a stray dog that hung around their house in Baile Olanesti in central Romania. She had grown fond of the mutt and had given it the name of Nusa.

On May 26, 2004, Livia was leaning over the balcony on the third floor of their home, cheerily ignoring her grandmother's admonition not to feed the dog, when she leaned out too far and fell.

Her grandmother, Jeni Ungureanu, seventy-seven, who had looked away after warning Livia not to throw any more food to the stray animal, ran to the balcony and saw her granddaughter lying on the ground. Immediately, she thought the worst. Her beloved, strong-willed Livia was either dead or severely injured.

Then she saw the dog struggling to get out from under Livia. The four-year-old had fallen on the dog, and it had cushioned her fall. With renewed hope sending energy into her legs, Jeni ran out to the street to gather her granddaughter into anxious arms.

Doctors at the local hospital pronounced Livia extremely fortunate to have suffered only minor injuries. On the same day, a village veterinarian gave Nusa a clean bill of health as well.

Jeni Ungureanu clearly recognized a miracle when she saw it. And she also agreed to permit Livia to keep Nusa as a pet.

he summer of 1990 provided quite a vacation for the Williamson family of New Zealand. Trudi, their eighteen-month-old rottweiler, had given birth to a batch of puppies. Now they were cruising along the scenic New Zealand coast in a forty-five-foot boat, delightedly watching dolphins dancing among the waves.

Tragically, while the family focused their attention on the surfacing and plunging marine mammals, Trudi, exhausted from her recent labors, fell overboard. In all the excitement of attending the boat and observing the dolphins at play, several hours passed before twelve-year-old Aaron noticed that his pet was missing.

Robert Williamson turned the craft around at his son's first outcry. They searched and searched; but when darkness came, they were forced to head for land.

Later that night, Robert heard his son's weeping and listened to his desperate prayers for a miracle to bring Trudi back to him.

The next day, Robert tried to explain the somber facts of life to his hopeful son. There really was no chance that Trudi had survived the sea. They had no choice but to return home with her orphaned puppies.

Two weeks later, however, Aaron would receive his miracle. A group of fishermen spotted the rottweiler on an uninhabitable rocky island. When they found the Williamsons' telephone number on Trudi's dog tags, they summoned the joyous, but astonished, father and son to come claim their pet.

Veterinary surgeon Murray Gibb agreed that Trudi's survival and rescue definitely fell within the category of miracles. The doctor theorized that extra body fat acquired during her pregnancy enabled Trudi to resist the numbing cold of the ocean and helped her to stay afloat during an eight-mile swim to the rocky island.

Once on land, however, the rottweiler found nothing to eat. She had subsisted without food for two weeks until she was found by the fishermen and returned to her family.

While Trudi the rottweiler had to swim for an island or perish at sea, Coco, a three-and-a-half-year-old Chow mix, was rescued after three days adrift on a twenty-nine-foot cabin cruiser. On August 13, 1998, Mike Palmer of Clearwater, Florida, had gone fishing for sponge and found the castaway canine instead.

Coco's owners, Julie Parsons and Andrew Block, had been taking a shower on the back of the cruiser when it hit a wave with such force that they were thrown overboard. The boat was in gear, so it kept moving ahead, leaving Coco staring back at Julie and Andrew as if they had gone suddenly crazy.

Although they were concerned about their dog, Julie and Andrew now had a serious problem of their own: They had been cast into the ocean without life vests or any kind of floatation equipment. They treaded water and swam for twenty-one hours before a Coast Guard crew on a training mission spotted them. Once they had been retrieved from the sea, Julie and Andrew explained about the plight of Coco and their cabin cruiser.

Hundreds of people in boats and two planes went searching for the missing dog and boat. All efforts seemed to be in vain until Palmer came upon the cruiser twenty-two miles out in the Gulf of Mexico, northwest of Tampa. The sponge fisherman said that as he approached the cruiser, he could see a dog standing out on the dive platform. When he managed to retrieve the dog, Palmer gave Coco a quart of water and called the authorities to see that the boat and the dog were returned to their thankful owners.

Trudi had her island, Coco his cabin cruiser, but poor little Nemo, a water-soaked kitten, had nothing but the sea in Homosassa Bay, three miles out in the Gulf of Mexico.

On July 8, 2004, a group of friends on a scalloping trip spotted a nine-inch-long kitten paddling all alone in the bay. Maggie Rogers—the director of finances at the Clearwater Marine Aquarium, and one of the people in the group of friends—told Eileen Schulte of the Saint Petersburg Times that they scooped up the kitten, which was crying at the top of its lungs, out of the water and that she held it in her lap for the rest of the day. There was no clue as to how the kitten had gotten three miles out to sea.

After the group returned to shore, the ten-week-old, one-pound-six-ounce kitten was proclaimed fit by a veterinarian and adopted by Ms. Rogers' sister-in-law. Unanimously, it was decided that the kitten should be named Nemo.

In July 1991, fifty-eight-year-old Shirley Smith of Bellevue, Ohio, had just returned from a week's stay in the hospital where she was diagnosed as suffering from congestive heart failure and failing lungs. The family cocker spaniel, Honey Bran Muffin IV, had long since been adapted to Mrs. Smith's physical limitations of deafness and blindness, but now he seemed to become immediately cognizant of his mistress's new condition.

During the night, Shirley awoke, unable to breathe and gasping for air. She knew that she was choking to death.

Awakened by the terrible sounds of gasping and distress, Muffin seemed to assess the seriousness of the situation and conclude that his master, Dallas Smith, was at a loss as to how to help Shirley through the trauma. Wasting not a second of crucial time, Muffin ran upstairs where the Smiths' thirty-year-old daughter, Karen, a medically trained respiratory therapist, lay sleeping.

Resentful of the intrusion into her sleep, Karen tried to shoo away the cocker spaniel. Irritated by the dog's nudges, she felt that Muffin had picked the very worst time to be playful.

When at last the determined Muffin's actions kept Karen from falling back asleep, the young woman became alert to the dog's intentions, and she heard the unmistakable sounds of a person choking. And in this particular instance, that person just happened to be her mother.

Karen rushed to her mother's room and employed her expertise and an inhaler to get Shirley breathing normally again.

There was no doubt in the mind of any member of the Smith family that Muffin had sensed that there was something drastically wrong with Shirley and had saved her life by awakening Karen to the danger.

ara Savick remem-
bered the Easter when
she was nine-years-old
and the Easter Bunny brought her a tiny duckling in a
yellow basket.

"Its downy little feathers were coarse because the
duckling had been dyed a sickening pink," Sara recalled.
"Mom said later that she bought the little duck because
she felt sorry for it. Without any great display of origi-
nality or creativity, I named the duck Pinky."

To the surprise of Sara's parents—and the delight
of Sara—Pinky grew and prospered. Within a couple
of months, the scrawny little pink-colored duckling had

become a healthy duck with white feathers and an enormous appetite.

"We fed Pinky oatmeal—cooked and uncooked—and bits of vegetables finely chopped," Sara said. "Although some people have doubted me on this claim, we did potty-train Pinky to use a newspaper on the porch. She might not always have made it to her designated potty place, but at least there weren't too many huge mistakes all over the house."

And Pinky had the run of the house. "She waddled and quacked wherever she pleased, upstairs and downstairs," Sara said. "And she loved to join me in the bathtub."

Just when everything seemed perfect, there came the night of 'the talk.'

"After dinner one night, Dad and Mom told me that it would be best for Pinky if she were allowed to join other ducks and live a normal duck-life," Sara said. "Ducks, Dad reminded me, are not usually found living indoors with families. Ducks are meant to be outside, waddling and quacking in ponds with other ducks and doing all the normal things that ducks did when they were together."

Sara remembered that tears were streaming down her cheeks. Although she was only nine, she could see where this conversation was headed. Besides, she had earlier that week overheard her mother exclaiming that she had never expected Pinky to live longer than a few days. Just long enough to celebrate the Easter holiday. Now, here it was, nearly five months later.

Mom and Dad suggested that they all take Pinky to join the other ducks in the pond at City Park. Here Pinky would be happy with the other boy and girl ducks, and Sara could come to visit her as often as she wished.

"I was grateful for one thing," Sara said. "At first I thought they were going to suggest that we eat Pinky. My friend Arthur told me that his parents had told him that his pet rabbit had run away but that he had been suspicious about the meat that his mother served for dinner one night. He had thrown a fit and been sent to his room."

The next day was a Sunday, and Sara and her parents put Pinky in a box and drove her to the park.

"Pinky seemed none too happy with my parents' plan that she should suddenly be transformed into a duck," Sara said. "It seemed obvious to me that Pinky thought she was a person and that she believed herself to be one of our family members. After all, we were the only family that she had ever known. I have since read that ducks will even adopt a boat as their mom if that is what they see 'swimming' near them in the water when they are first hatched. And Pinky wasn't too long out of the egg when the Easter Bunny brought her to our house."

Sara remembered that even her father kind of teared up when they left Pinky at the pond and headed back toward the car.

"'She'll be fine,' Dad kept saying over and over, reassuring himself as well as me," Sara said. "Mom was absolutely silent, and I knew that she would start to cry if she said one word. I looked over my shoulder at Pinky standing morosely apart from the other ducks, who were just swimming around in circles, looking at her as if she had suddenly arrived from another planet of alien ducks."

When Sara was getting ready for school the next morning, she glanced out of the kitchen window and nearly spilled her glass of orange juice in her excitement. Pinky was back, contentedly rummaging in the grass in the backyard, deftly snatching up any worms and insects that fell prey to her beak.

"Pinky had traveled over two miles, crossed three intersections with heavy traffic, and cheerily left the ducks to be reunited with her human family," Sara said. "Tears filled my eyes when I visualized Pinky dodging in and out of traffic unable to fly above the cars and trucks because Dad had clipped her wings. I hadn't fussed or cried (well, not too much) when we took Pinky to the park to be with the other ducks, but this time I really screeched and raised a rumpus. Pinky wanted to be with us. She didn't want to be with the ducks at City Park pond."

✿ ✿ ✿ *Pet Miracles* ✿ ✿ ✿

Sara's tears and tantrums were to no avail. When she refused to go to school that day, her father put her and Pinky in the car and drove them to their respective destinations.

"Dad carried Pinky to the pond and stood for a few moments, telling her to 'stay' as if she were a dog," Sara said. "I cried all the way to school, then told the school nurse that I had an upset stomach so I could lie down in her office and manage to stop crying."

The next morning, Pinky was once again foraging in the backyard.

"How does she do it?" Sara's father asked, waving his arms wildly and casting his eyes skyward. "How does she manage to waddle and fly back home through all that traffic without getting hit?"

He bent to pick Pinky up to put her in the box so that he could once again return her to the City Park. Then he straightened himself upright and tossed the box against the backyard fence. Clearly, he was torn, trying desperately to decide what was the right thing to do.

Sara remembered pleading Pinky's case: "Daddy, Pinky knows her home is with us. She wants to live with us, not some old ducks. She loves us. I love her. I know you and Mommy do, too. Please let her stay. Please—or she'll just get hit by a car some night when she's coming home to us. Do you want Pinky to get hit by a truck?"

That was when Sara lost control of her passionate advocacy of the case for allowing Pinky to stay with the family that she had come to love. "I just started to cry," she said. "I knelt beside Pinky and stroked her back and cried. Then I saw that Daddy had dropped his arms to his sides and Mommy was hugging him. They both had tears in their eyes."

Pinky lived with Sara and her family for nearly four years. "Pinky had a good life with us," Sara said. "She loved us, and we loved her. One morning when I came downstairs to get ready to go to school, I walked over to Pinky's cage on the porch to give her a handful of oatmeal. When she didn't respond, I felt the coldness of her body and tearfully realized that she had gone home to the Great Duck Pond somewhere in the beyond. We conducted a funeral service and buried her in the back-yard. Mom planted some tulip bulbs that would bloom every Easter in memory of Pinky."

*M*any men and women who suffer from various diseases and illnesses have observed how aware their pets become of their infirmities and how these animals come to play a protective role in their lives. In the mid-1970s, tests were conducted in Great Britain in which the mentally ill were given a pet to look after. After a brief period of time, many patients showed an impressive degree of recovery. Several were able to resume their place in the outside world and once again to lead stable lives.

It has often been conjectured that pets can sense both the mental and physical weaknesses of their owners and will endeavor to do the best they can to supplement those disabilities. Glen W. wrote to tell us the time when his family's Standard Poodle, Pierre, came to the rescue of his mentally retarded younger brother.

Although Pierre certainly had his own personality, Glen said, he was by no means a trained or uniquely talented dog. Glen could get him to "speak" if he held Pierre's food dish over his head long enough, and he looked alert when Glen shouted, "sic 'em!" Those were the only "tricks" that Pierre knew.

"Pierre also had a habit of lying in the middle of a rather busy two-lane street near our house and making traffic go around him," Glen added. "He was quite well known in the neighborhood for this accomplishment."

At the time of the incident in which Pierre displayed his true inner mettle, Glen was thirteen and his brother was around eight years old. Although his brother seemed always contented to remain in the fenced-in backyard, on this particular day, he opened the gate and wandered out for a walk. Glen's three-year-old niece decided to go along. Fortunately for them, so did Pierre, for the two youngsters were soon a half a mile away at the intersection of a busy four-lane street.

Glen was in the front yard, oblivious, along with the rest of the family, to the whereabouts of his brother and niece when a man drove up to their house and called to him. Puzzled, Glen walked to the fence and heard what the driver had to say.

"He asked if we owned a big black dog," Glen recalled. "I admitted that we did, and then he told me that our dog and a couple of kids were down on the four-lane street attempting to cross it. He emphasized that there was no cross walk or traffic light in the vicinity."

Glen's mom joined him at the fence and heard the man say that the big black dog wouldn't allow the kids to cross the street. "The dog also won't let anyone approach them," he said. "I know, because I tried to get the kids in my car to bring them back here."

Shaking with fear and dread, Glen's mother and grandmother got into their car and drove down to retrieve his brother and niece.

"Pierre got to walk home," Glen said, "because he was always in need of a bath."

Glen concluded by stating that Pierre never again exhibited any such dramatically heroic behavior. Although others might not consider the action of the poodle miraculous, Glen remembered the dog's intervention on behalf of his brother and niece as an "amazing event" from his childhood.

imbo, a five-year-old German shepherd, was blinded and burned beyond recognition in an explosion that followed the devastating Los Angeles earthquake in January 1994. Although her owner, Jim Menzi, first assumed that his dog had been consumed by the flames, she miraculously survived the deadly inferno.

Jim's truck had stalled at an intersection flooded by a broken water main during those frightening moments after the quake. His two canine buddies, Shep and Bimbo, were with him in the cab when he tried once again to start his vehicle.

Jim did not know that there was a natural gas leak that had been caused by the tremors of the deadly quake, and when he turned the key in the ignition, the gas connected with the spark and exploded.

Instinctively, Jim jumped from his burning truck and into the water that surrounded it. He assumed that his dogs would follow his lead and abandon ship, but when he heard their terrible wails and yelps of pain and fear, he realized that the flames were holding them back.

Sadly, helpless to do anything to help them escape, all Jim Menzi could do was to pray that Shep and Bimbo would die as quickly and as painlessly as possible.

Later that day, when he was taken to a hospital, it was discovered that Jim had burns on 30 percent of his body. As he was rushed to intensive care, he mourned his dogs' fate. He said later that he kept replaying in his mind the nightmare explosion that had claimed his dogs' lives. He could still hear their pathetic howls, and he cried for them.

But three days later, Jim received the astonishing news that Bimbo had somehow managed to survive the fire in the pickup. She had been found temporarily blind and completely helpless, wandering in someone's yard, by a fireman who then took her to a veterinarian. Unfortunately, it was certain that Shep died in the fire.

From his hospital bed, Jim called the vet and inquired about his beloved Bimbo's well-being. The German shepherd had sustained burns covering nearly 70 percent of her body. She would have to continue to fight to live.

Jim gave thought to the humane consideration that it might be better to put her to sleep—but the confident veterinarian reminded him that the doctors at the hospital had not put him to sleep.

Inspired by the vet's positive attitude, Jim resolved that he would not allow Bimbo to die. He arranged to talk to his dog via a speakerphone, and he told Bimbo that he loved her. The nurse with the German shepherd at the Blue Cross Pet Hospital said that every time Jim spoke, Bimbo licked her hand.

Both master and dog underwent similar treatments for their burns. After sixteen days in the hospital, Jim was released, and he immediately headed for the pet hospital to be with Bimbo.

The attending veterinarians had shaved what patches of hair had not been burned in the pickup fire, and her paws were swollen and bleeding, but to Jim Menzi's eyes, Bimbo had never looked more beautiful.

Later, Jim said that he had never felt a stronger bond with his dog. He believed that he and Bimbo had been given a second chance at life, and the two of them were going to live each day for all it was worth.

Seventy-two-year-old Graham Bailey was feeding his four South American llamas—Milo, Bertie, Horatio, and Felix—on his farm near Kettering, Northants, United Kingdom, when he stepped in a rabbit hole and wrenched his leg and hip. Bailey felt great pain, and he could tell that he had injured himself severely. He extricated himself from the hole, but he found that he could not stand. He was about 100 yards from a road, and he knew that he would have to crawl to find help.

Bailey used the llamas to protect his flocks of sheep from foxes and dogs, particularly during the lambing season. He was pleased with the serious manner in which the llamas guarded the sheep, so he was not surprised when the llamas drew near to protect him as he crawled across the field.

For two hours, Bailey painfully made his way toward the road. A lady walking her dog heard his cries for help and called for an ambulance. Within a short time, the paramedics arrived and entered the field to come to Bailey's aid.

Unfortunately, the llamas had no way of knowing that the people approaching their injured master were coming to help him. In their capacity as guard animals, they viewed the strange people in yellow jackets running toward the farmer as belonging to the same threatening category as foxes and marauding dogs. Milo, the llamas' leader, became very excited about the paramedics invading the field, and he directed the other three to form a tight circle around Bailey.

Bailey told the paramedics that it would be all right to approach, but the rescue workers were concerned that the nervously dancing animals would charge them. Every time they attempted to reach Bailey, Milo would stir the others up into agitated movements that looked to the paramedics suspiciously like attack mode. In desperation, they put a call into the Diana Princess of Wales Air Ambulance Service to perform a low fly-over to frighten away the llamas.

✿ ✿ *Pet Miracles* ✿ ✿

While Milo and his fellow guardians felt great confidence in their ability to keep the paramedics at bay, the helicopter's sudden powerful and noisy presence in the sky caused them to retreat to the far end of the pasture long enough for the ambulance crew to place Bailey on a stretcher and remove him from the field. The farmer was taken to the Kettering General Hospital where he was treated for a fractured hip.

Bailey expressed his apologies for causing the rescue workers so much trouble, but he explained once again that Milo, Bertie, Horatio, and Felix took their job as guard llamas very seriously. He was not at all surprised that the llamas had come to protect him and that they had stood guard over him as he painfully made his way to help.

On April 18, 2004, the Schwartz family of Trona, California, was hiking near the ghost town of Panamint City, on the western edge of Death Valley National Park, when their dog Shadow fell into a pit. The chasm was so deep that they could not see Shadow, but they could hear her whimpering so they knew that she was still alive and had survived the fall.

The pit was four feet wide, but the Schwartzs could not determine its depth. They found an aluminum ladder at a nearby ranger station and attempted to rescue their ten-year-old cocker spaniel-beagle friend from the hole. They planned to lower the ladder to the bottom of the pit and then descend to retrieve Shadow. When they accidentally dropped the ladder and it fell out of reach, they realized that the pit was much deeper than they had estimated.

Seventeen-year-old Stephen continued to call to Shadow, but finally the dog ceased responding. After a family counsel, Stephen's father, brother, and two cousins decided that Shadow had died. The pit had to be thirty or more feet in depth. Poor old Shadow had probably received fatal injuries from the fall and had just managed to hang on for several minutes more. The Schwartzs fashioned a wooden cross to mark Shadow's final resting place, said a prayer in memory of their faithful friend, and sadly returned home.

On May 16, five weeks after the Schwartz family believed that they had lost Shadow to an abyss in the desert, brothers Darren and Scott Mertz were looking for the source of a spring near Panamint City. They stopped to rest near a deep pit with a wooden cross over it. They were daring one another to climb down inside the hole when they were startled to hear barking coming from its darkened depths.

Horrified to hear what sounded like a dog down in the pit, the brothers resolved not to leave until they had rescued it. Thirty-four-year-old Darren used an old hose from a nearby water storage tank to lower Scott, thirty-six, down to the ladder that the Schwartzs had lost in their attempt to rescue Shadow. Scott descended further until he reached a very frightened and skinny dog. Although the dog was obviously malnourished, Scott observed that water at the bottom of the chasm had allowed the animal to survive. Darren and Scott had no idea that Shadow had been at the bottom of the pit for thirty-five days.

Later, when they returned to Scott's home in Temecula and had given the dog some food and water, the brothers called the number on her tags and told the Schwartz family that they had retrieved their dog from a pit in the desert.

An astonished Stephen could hardly believe that Shadow was still alive after the family had left her for dead five weeks before. He admitted that he had prayed for such a miracle and had asked that he would once again see Shadow alive. After all, his prayers would be answered, and the beloved dog would be returned to the family a few pounds lighter, but in good health.

Judy, a ten-month-old terrier, survived an astounding thirty-six days trapped underground in a rabbit hole.

It had begun as an ordinary afternoon walk around the family farm for eleven-year-old Evan Davies on a summer's day in 1990. Judy was dashing ahead in the field near the Davies' home in Powys, Wales. Spotting a rabbit, the feisty terrier pursued the bunny to its "front door"—as she so often did—but this time she went right on inside Mr. Rabbit's home.

Evan was left standing there, open-mouthed with shock. Judy had often chased the rabbits to their holes, then bounded away to find new game when the long-eared creatures disappeared into their warrens, but she had never before taken her pursuit to the rabbits' private domain.

Evan called and called for his pet to return, then ran off sobbing to enlist the help of his mother and sister. That night, after work, Evan's father joined the search for the missing dog.

The eleven-year-old boy maintained his faithful vigil for his beloved terrier for several days, and his parents tried to console him with promises of obtaining another Judy.

Blinking back his tears, Evan stoutly insisted that there could never be another Judy and that he knew that somehow she was still alive.

A month later, Malcolm Davies asked his son if he would reconsider the offer of a new puppy. He explained that there was no way that Judy would ever come back to him now, and that Evan had to face the sad truth of the matter.

Evan knew that his father meant well, but he asked everyone to wait a little longer. Judy might show up, he said, more as a plea than an assertion.

Incredibly, it was only a week later that John Gordon, one of the Davies's neighbors, was awakened at midnight by the sound of a dog barking. Somehow Gordon knew that it was Evan's missing terrier.

About half a mile from his home, Gordon found a skinny, half-starved dog attempting to claw its way out of a rabbit hole. He dug the terrier free with his bare hands, and gave her some food and water. He permitted her only a few moments of rest, and then he put her in his car and drove her home to the Davies's farm.

Malcolm and his wife awakened their son with the joyful news that Judy had returned from her thirty-six-day sojourn in the kingdom of the rabbits. Evan jumped from his bed, laughing and sobbing in uncontrollable delight.

Later, an examining veterinarian found that except for a minor eye infection, Judy was surprisingly none the worse for wear after her five-week ordeal. He theorized that the stubborn terrier managed to survive on her own body fat, perhaps a slaughtered rabbit, plant roots, and insects. She must also have found some underground water.

Evans set about fattening up his remarkable pet so that Judy would become so plump she wouldn't be able to squeeze down any more rabbit holes.

✿ ✿ *Pet Miracles* ✿ ✿

On a hot day in July 2003, Chris Nelson saw a dog under the floorboards of the senior center in Grants Pass, Oregon, which was being reconstructed at the time. Nelson had crawled under the building because a security officer reported whimpering sounds coming from the construction site. The center had burned down a couple of months before, and efforts to rebuild it had begun. If there was a dog under the floorboards, the poor thing would have to have been there for a long time.

Nelson confirmed that the security officer had not been hearing things. There was a dog whimpering for help under the floorboards of the senior center. A dog that had endured extreme heat without water or food for nearly three weeks. He said that she was nothing but skin and bones.

Nelson crawled inside a small opening with a bowl of water for the dog and began speaking to her very quietly. She was in a small space three or four feet from the floor to the cement to the floorboard. Temperatures had climbed to over 100 degrees, and very little air was coming through the plastic vents to the space. Somehow, the dog had managed to survive under seemingly impossible conditions.

Six hours later, thanks to the combined efforts of police, firefighters, and two members of the construction crew, the dog—whom Nelson named Phoenix—was rescued from the dark, tomblike enclosure. Someone recognized the dog and said that her owners had called her Buttercup, but Nelson's fellow rescuers sided with his choice of a new name.

The veterinarians treating Phoenix agreed that her survival under the floorboards for such a long time was a miracle. Although Dr. Rebecca Hall said that the three-year-old hound was one of the thinnest dogs that she had ever treated, Phoenix was soon thriving on nutritional support and high grains. She spent a week at the clinic before being reclaimed by her owners.

In the winter of 2002, a thief in Vologada, Russia, fancied and attempted to steal an attractive fur hat from the head of a gentleman passerby. The thief received instant and fierce retribution when the fur collar of the victim's coat sunk its teeth and claws into him. What had at first appeared to be a luxuriant collar was actually a Siamese cat, and the would-be fur-snatcher soon fled in pain and terror.

The cat's owner explained that he had taken his pet along on his walk as an added protection against the freezing cold weather. He had no idea that the Siamese would also provide protection against thieves, but he

did observe that there were few animals more frightening than an angry cat.

From our friend, Paul Bannister, an experienced
journalist of many years experience, comes the story of
a dynamic duo—stranger than Batman and Robin—in
the war against drugs and crime. A few years ago, Bannister encountered the bizarre partnership of forty-one-
year-old Erika (an undercover name adopted by James
Lewis) and his sidekick, Baby, the raccoon.

Some years ago, Lewis declared a vendetta against
the hardened drug dealers in the Houston neighborhood
where he lived. Dressing as a woman and assuming the
personality of "Erika," the determined crimefighter had,
at first, carried a .44 Colt handgun in his purse. When
his sidearm was stolen, Wilson began carrying Baby, his
pet raccoon, with him.

Whenever thugs threatened him, Lewis told Bannister,
he simply shoved Baby in their faces and that always
scared them off. Although it is unlikely that in even his
wildest raccoon dreams Baby ever envisioned himself as a
bodyguard for a cross-dressing crime fighter, he appeared
to have the necessary muscle to send fear into the hearts
of hardened drug pushers. According to Lewis, many a
tough guy had been rocked back on his heels when Baby,
the raccoon, was brandished in his face.

When Wilson spoke to journalist Bannister, he claimed that he had already collared twenty drug peddlers for the Houston police. "I tell them, you may as well move on," Lewis said. "The Raccoon Lady is here—and the cops won't be far behind. Baby and I won't stop until we have driven all of these people out of our neighborhood."

According to what Bannister learned, Baby and Erika staked out the abandoned houses where crack dealers hung out. Then they boldly walked in and told the hoodlums that it was time for them to hit the road.

The police would come when he called, Lewis said, because he did not call as a victim reporting a crime. He told police, "Come and take away this drug dealer I've found."

Bannister interviewed a Houston police officer, who confirmed that the Raccoon Lady and "her" sidekick had called in the authorities to arrest drug dealers on numerous occasions. However, the officer emphasized that they did not recommend that the public go into crack houses the way the Raccoon Lady and Baby did. What they were doing was far too dangerous.

Another Houston police officer admitted that the two bizarre crime-busters went into a lot of places where police officers couldn't go. What Erika and Baby did was dangerous, he said, but they got the arrests because of it.

*F*orty-one-year-old Samuel Green-field of Marietta, Georgia, had broken his back twice and now walks with a cane. Perhaps his physical condition helped him to feel great empathy when, a few years back he found a female Labrador mix badly injured in his yard.

It was apparent to Greenfield that she had been struck by a car and had managed to crawl to safety on his property. Since she had no license or identification tags, it was also apparent that the injured dog was a stray.

Greenfield patiently and lovingly nursed the dog, whom he named Lucy, back to health, and the two became inseparable.

In May 1998, when Greenfield was heading back to his car after stopping at a market for a few groceries, two hoodlums approached him and demanded his wallet and his watch. Lucy, who was inside the car, began to bark fiercely.

Greenfield managed to use the walking stick as a weapon, and he knocked one of the thugs out cold.

But his act of defiance sent the other hood into a rage, and the would-be mugger began to hit Greenfield with violent, powerful blows. As his assailant spun him around against the car, Greenfield thought that a knife in his ribs would probably be his fate.

Somehow, though, Greenfield managed to reach out and open the car door. Lucy hurled herself from within and struck the thug full in the chest, knocking him to the ground.

Greenfield could clearly see the terror in his attacker's eyes as the Labrador's bared teeth snapped scant inches from his face.

The thug managed to push the dog off him, and he took off running, with Lucy barking and snapping at his heels.

As Greenfield limped toward the store to call for help, the punk that he had knocked cold regained consciousness, and looked around at a very different scene— one in which he and his partner were the victims—and he, too, ran off.

When Samuel Greenfield returned from making his call to the police, Lucy was heading back to the car with a definite air of triumph exuding from her confident trot. As he hugged her to his chest, Greenfield thanked her for returning the favor. She had now saved his life as he had saved hers—and the two of them would be inseparable friends for as long as the good Lord blessed them.

*A*s researchers of the strange and the unknown, as well as the miraculous and the angelic, we have related a number of personal experiences in which our pets were sensitive to the vibrations of ghosts in so-called haunted houses. In one instance, however, our dog Simba seemed to pick up on vibrations of evil from thousands of miles away.

We had been conducting a telephone interview with the rugged actor Clint Walker, star of *Cheyenne*, a popular television series of the 1950s, and such motion pictures as *The Dirty Dozen* (1967) and *The White Buffalo* (1977). He had been telling us about a mysterious attack he had weathered from four eerie dogs that had seemingly manifested from nowhere. Walker had been recovering from a serious accident that had nearly claimed his life, and he said that the creatures seemed to sense his vulnerability. The dogs—if that is what they were—were strange looking creatures, like no dogs he had ever seen before.

Although he had managed to drive the dogs away, that night he had experienced an awful nightmare which required him to set his willpower against the dream's power and to call upon the name of Jesus to reject its negative energy.

"There are evil forces, you know," Clint told us. "I have learned this is so, and we must stay strong against them and not give them power over us."

As the actor had been completing his eerie tale, Simba, our old Lhasa apso, a fellow 'way up in doggy years, began to growl and bark at something in our darkened hallway.

We were both very startled by his loud barking, for truly, Simba never barked at anything. With the exception of a sharp yip when it was time to obey a call of nature, he was very nearly mute. And now, he was growling and walking very cautiously toward something that he could sense or see in the dark corner of the hallway.

When our interview was concluded, we left our office to investigate the hallway, but we found nothing. Simba, however, continued his nervous growling and his fixation on one particular spot in the hallway. He continued his vigil for nearly an hour until whatever it was that he perceived on some level of his consciousness had dissipated.

Had Simba somehow picked up on our conversation and in some manner received an image of those devil dogs that had attacked Clint Walker? Or had our conversation about the eerie and demonic brought some negative influence, some evil energy, temporarily into our own home?

Whatever it was, we had the courageous Simba to keep it at bay.

*C*iak, a German shep-
herd-collie mix,
found himself in a
most peculiar situation. His owner's cleaning lady had
taken him for a walk and for whatever reason, Ciak
decided to run away.

His problem was that once he had run a good distance
away from his mistress's cleaning lady, Ciak discovered
that he was not one of those dogs who had the ability to
find his way home across mountains, icy rivers, and mam-
moth canyons. The stark reality was that he couldn't find
his way through the streets of Rome to return his mistress,
Italian anchorwoman Alessandra Canale.

Ciak finally made his way across the Eternal City and ended up at the front door of Monica Nannini, an actress, who took pity on the stray pooch and invited him into her home. The confused Ciak unhesitatingly accepted her hospitality, and he made himself comfortable in this place of refuge for over thirty days.

From the very beginning of his sojourn, Monica noticed that Ciak seemed to behave very strangely whenever a certain attractive blonde newscaster appeared on the television screen. He would immediately begin to bark and wag his tail. The actress laughingly assumed that the stray mutt had a thing for Alessandra Canale.

Interestingly, Monica knew Alessandra casually, but she had no idea that the newsperson had lost a dog or that she even owned a dog.

About a month after Ciak had moved in with her, the actress happened to run into the anchorwoman at a bar near the television studio. Jokingly, Monica told her about the stray dog's behavior whenever Alessandra appeared on the television screen. Either the dog had a crush on Alessandra or maybe his former owner had long blonde hair like hers.

Alessandra became very excited. She explained that she had lost a dog of the same German shepherd-collie mix that Monica described. She had searched the neighborhood for her missing companion, and she had placed posters in local stores and taken out ads in the newspapers. All without success.

The television personality said that she had accepted the sad fate that Ciak had been put to sleep, since stray dogs are only kept for twenty-fours by animal shelters in Rome.

Monica invited Alessandra to come home with her and to have a look at her canine admirer.

Later, Alessandra told journalist Silvio Piersanti that she had known as soon as Monica described the dog that it had to be her dear Ciak. She said that she couldn't wait to put her arms around her beloved dog. As soon as Monica opened the door, Ciak jumped on Alessandra, almost knocking her down, and licked her face. The actress and the anchorwoman agreed that it was a wonderful reunion.

She had only managed to get a few miles out of town when Kathie heard a strange popping sound in the engine of the truck she had just purchased that day. As she was trying to identify the source of the sudden series of explosions, the steering wheel twisted violently and she almost lost her grip on it. Eve, Kathie's six-year-old rottweiler, tumbled off the seat as Kathie struggled to regain control of the fishtailing vehicle. At last, she managed to bring the truck to a screeching stop at the side of the road.

Fortunately, there had been hardly any traffic that winter's night in January 1992, when Kathie and Eve had set out from their home in Indiana to attend an antique show in Atlanta. Kathie sighed with relief as she thought about what could have happened to her and her dog if she had swerved into oncoming traffic or been rear-ended as she was suddenly forced to brake.

Although forty-one-year-old Kathie had been paralyzed from the waist down for six years from the effects of multiple sclerosis, she maintained excellent upper body strength. That power and mobility had just come into serious play when she was forced to re-establish control of the truck that had, for some reason, experienced a serious engine malfunction.

Eve licked at Kathie's hand, needing some assurance that her mistress was all right. Kathie continued to sit in stunned silence, collecting her thoughts.

Kathie reached over and rubbed Eve's head affectionately. Something serious was wrong with the vehicle, but at least they were both uninjured. It could have been a lot worse if they had struck another vehicle or spun around and tipped over.

Suddenly, to Kathie's horror, she saw—and smelled— that the cab was filling with foul black smoke. The truck was on fire!

Kathie had a clear image of the truck bursting into a fireball that would consume both Eve and herself. She opened the door on the driver's side and told Eve to get out.

When the big rottweiler hesitated to leave her, Kathie shoved her out the door. Then she grabbed the frame of her wheelchair and threw it out after the dog.

Kathie experienced a moment of panic when she could not find the wheels of her chair in all the smoke. She began coughing and choking as the dense smoke intensified in the cab of the truck. Frantically, her desperate fingers searched for the wheels, but the noxious fumes continued to disorient her. The only thought that remained clear was the grim realization that the truck was about to explode with her in it. Kathie could hardly breathe. Her vision began to fade and her fear became overwhelming.

Then she became aware of the 104-pound rottweiler trying to clutch her arm with its teeth. Kathie had expected the dog's natural fear of fire and smoke to make Eve run away from the truck, but she could feel the dog trying to pull her out.

Just before Kathie blacked out, she felt Eve grab her right leg and tug her free of the cab. Once free of the truck and lying on the pavement, Kathie flickered in and out of consciousness, and she was dimly aware of Eve's jaws clamped around her ankle as the faithful rottweiler dragged her away from the truck.

Eve had managed to pull Kathie about ten feet away from the truck when the two of them were rocked by a loud explosion. Flames swallowed the cab, and leaped eight feet into the air.

Recovering from the shock of the blast, Eve continued pulling Kathie toward the more complete safety of a nearby ditch. The rottweiler was undistracted by the flames and the smoke, and she concentrated on the priority of seeing that Kathie was safe.

It wasn't until Eve released her ankle that Kathie regained enough consciousness to realize fully what a courageous thing her beloved rottweiler had accomplished. Eve had fearlessly pulled Kathie to safety at the risk of her own life.

The downside of Kathie's recovering more complete consciousness was her growing awareness of the pain in her head and ribs. She knew that she was going to require medical attention.

Kathie was relieved when a patrol car arrived on the scene, and an officer began to run toward her to offer assistance. But the rottweiler, hypersensitive to all the chaos and danger that she and her mistress had just endured, assumed a protective stance over Kathie and would not permit the patrolman to approach them.

The police office told Kathie had he had radioed for an ambulance and a fire truck, but that she had to get farther away from the truck at once. The gas tank could explode at any second—and the fiery blast would easily reach the spot where she lay protected by her dog.

Startled by the knowledge of this new danger, Kathie desperately began to pull herself toward the officer and the patrol car.

It took Eve only a moment to assess the new situation and the new challenge. She bent low to offer Kathie her collar and dragged her an additional forty feet to safety.

Whether due to the efforts of the firefighters or the result of a quirk of fate, the gas tank did not explode. Kathie recalled that it took the firefighters some time to extinguish the burning truck.

As the chaos and the danger subsided at last, Eve permitted the patrolman to approach and pet her. He told Eve that she was an awfully good dog.

The paramedics assessed Kathie's injuries and determined them as minor, but recommended that she be more thoroughly examined by a doctor. When Kathie overheard the patrolman evaluate Eve as an "awfully good dog," she thought the compliment to be the understatement of the year.

In November, 1993, Ray Ellis was outside his home, using his chainsaw to cut fallen dead trees for firewood. Girl, his German shepherd, was having a good time scaring up rabbits in the wooded area about 250 yards from the Ellis home.

Seventy-four-year-old Ray was so intent on sawing through a dead tree limb he didn't notice the sapling trapped beneath it. As the chainsaw buzzed through the wood, the sapling snapped up and hit Ray in the forehead, knocking him unconscious. As he fell to the ground unconscious, he dropped the chainsaw, and it severed his left foot at the ankle.

Immediately, Girl realized that Ray was in serious trouble. Forgetting any other attractions the woods might have for her, Girl ran home to summon Ray's wife, Dorothy.

Dorothy said later that she let Girl in the house as soon as she heard the shepherd barking and scratching at the door with her paws. Once inside, Girl ran back and forth from the front door to the side door, barking all the while. Dorothy had never seen the dog behave in such a manner, so she opened the door and told Girl to go find Ray.

Girl ran the 250 yards to the scene of the accident in much shorter time than Dorothy took to cover the terrain. By the time Dorothy arrived at her husband's side and had rolled him over, she was horrified to see her husband bleeding badly. She told Girl to look after him, and then Dorothy ran back home to dial 911.

When rescue workers arrived on the scene, they found Girl lying at her master's side, whining softly and gently licking Ray's face.

Because of Girl's fast action in getting help for her injured owner, Ray got to the hospital quickly enough so that doctors were able to perform microsurgery and successfully reattach his severed foot. When Ray regained consciousness, he declared himself the luckiest man alive to have a friend like Girl.

In 1994, Girl was named Ken-L Ration Dog Hero of the Year for her immediate grasp of her owner's predicament and her rapid action in summoning assistance.

There must have been times when Rhonda McCrory of Kosciusko, Mississippi, wondered why she had even acquired her moody little Pomeranian, Buddy. No one else liked him—none of her friends and none of her family members. They all complained because of Buddy's grumpy, sour disposition. But on July 14, 2004, grouchy little Buddy became Rhonda McCrory's miracle.

As flames spread through the McCrorys' home, Buddy's shrill barking awakened Rhonda just in time so that she and her children could escape. When Rhonda looked in the kitchen as she ran out, all she could see was smoke and fire. She sent fourteen-year-old Megan and twelve-year-old Austin to a neighbor's home to call 911, and then she got the keys and backed her pickup out of the driveway before it, too, could catch fire.

Although firefighters arrived just four minutes after the call came in, Kosciusko Fire Chief Duane Burdine told Mark Thorton of *The Star Herald* that flames were already coming out of the front door and a window, and that the house was "60 percent involved."

As she sadly surveyed the charred ruins of their home once the fire was put out, Rhonda mused how everything a family had worked for all their lives could be gone "in the blink of an eye." Thankfully, the McCrorys did have insurance, so they were able to recoup their material losses.

On a positive note, Ms. McCrory knew that at least the family would have to change their minds about moody, grumpy Buddy. "He was my miracle," she said. "He saved our lives."

Forty-one-year-old Sandy Seltzer knew that something was terribly wrong when Morris, her guide dog, awakened her at 11:30 p.m. on February 7, 1995.

As she became more fully awake, Sandy smelled smoke and heard frightened and confused shouting. Soon after, she heard the wail of sirens and the sounds of fire trucks and emergency vehicles pulling up in front of her apartment building.

Morris was nudging her out of bed. The big Labrador was indicating as best he could that they had to get out of the place. The building was definitely on fire.

Blind since her college days, Sandy knew that getting down from the fifth floor of a burning apartment building would present a challenge to Morris, but she was confident that he could handle it.

Holding tightly onto his leash, Sandy followed Morris out to the hallway and then down the stairs. Sandy heard people shouting, some crying desperately, as they struggled against smoke, fire, and chaos to find their way to safety. There were eighty residents in the apartment house in Mineola, New York, and she prayed that everyone would escape the building unscathed.

When Morris reached the third floor, he halted their descent. The smoke was almost overpowering, and Sandy sensed that Morris was considering whether or not to further risk the stairs.

After a few moments of deliberation, Morris backed up and began to walk along the third floor hallway. He had made a decision that Mineola Fire Chief William Mahoney would later say took intelligence and courage.

About a dozen third-floor residents had been watching the guide dog as he considered whether or not to continue down the stairs. They, too, were undecided. Would they find their way to the street and safety—or would they walk directly into the flames and suffocating smoke of a raging inferno?

When Morris finally backed away, the men and women decided that "his nose knew," that he had somehow sensed danger ahead, and they followed behind Sandy and her guide dog.

Morris continued down the hallway and then abruptly halted his party of thirteen humans who were depending on him for their lives. He stood still as heavy, choking billows of smoke filled the hallway. Then, when he sensed that the firefighters had poured enough water on the floors below to make the flames subside, Morris led Sandy and the other residents down through the darkness to the street outside the apartment house.

Fire investigator Dominick Mazza agreed with Chief Mahoney in declaring Morris a true hero. Mazza told reporters that those residents on the third floor might not have survived if it hadn't been for Morris.

Both Sandy and her courageous guide dog required treatment for smoke inhalation, and, in all, fourteen tenants in the building suffered minor injuries. But there were no fatalities—thanks to the fast action of the Mineola firefighters and the bravery and steady nerves of a resourceful Labrador guide dog.

Sandy Seltzer, a singer and songwriter, was so proud of her courageous Morris that she said that she would absolutely spoil him with Milk Bones for the rest of his life.

*E*veryone knows that cats really don't have nine lives—but on some occasions it seems as though the ancient bit of folklore might really be true.

Fortunately, James Brown and Mary Darden were not home in April 1996, when an explosion completely demolished their house in Wilkinsburg, Pennsylvania. It may have been a faulty water heater or the furnace that somehow caused the terrible blast, which reduced the house to splinters.

When they arrived to investigate the rubble-strewn lot where their house had once stood, Mary found an egg, still intact, beside the charred refrigerator. Holding the egg in her hand, Mary offered a silent prayer that if the delicate shell of an egg could endure the horrendous blast, perhaps some miracle might have spared Jack, her beloved cat.

Four days later, a neighbor called Mary and told her to visit the site of her former home if she wanted to see a real, live miracle.

When she arrived at the site, she was overjoyed to see Jack, alive and with only minor injuries.

It is likely that Jack had been trapped in a pocket of debris and was forced to dig himself out. Most of his hair was seared off in the blast of the explosion, and he had injured a paw during the process of excavating himself. But Jack only had to cash in about seven of his nine lives, and so Mary found him atop the rubble, a little the worse for wear but intact nonetheless.

On March 29, 2004, a two-year-old cat named Billy was placed comfortably in his cage and put on a US Airways flight from Phoenix to Philadelphia. Here, the cat was ticketed for a connecting flight with his owners, Guenther and Ingrid Koelbl, who were homeward bound for Germany.

The problem was that Billy's cage was empty when the flight arrived in Philadelphia. The cat had escaped and apparently decided to follow unshared travel plans of his own. He could not be found anywhere on the plane, and officials of the airline were embarrassed to admit that it was as if Billy had simply disappeared.

Nineteen days later, Billy was found on the same US Airways plane at Manchester Airport in New Hampshire. Somehow, he had managed to evade baggage handlers and all those individuals searching for him, and scrounged enough food and water to survive in the baggage compartment of the plane. He was treated at an animal hospital for dehydration and released to his grateful owners.

In mid-April 2004, a cat jumped out of a container of parrot cages when the shipment arrived at Goldberg's warehouse in Tampa, Florida.

The metal container, sealed a month earlier in China, had arrived by boat in Los Angeles in early April and had been transferred to Tampa by rail. During the journey, the cat had chewed up a number of cardboard boxes that held the bird cages, but no trace of water or food could be found that would explain how the cat had managed to survive locked in a metal container for a month. Veterinarians who examined the cat and treated her for dehydration said that she would soon be ready for adoption.

In autumn of 1997, Vivian Browning of Damascus, Maryland, hired some workers to fill in a hole that had been left under her back porch by a pesky woodchuck. The seventy-three-year-old woman had no idea her beloved Tabby had been exploring the burrow when the men began dumping dirt into it, and the cat was trapped inside when the hole was sealed.

That night, when Tabby didn't come home, Vivian became very upset. Tabby was very precious to Vivian, and although sometimes Tabby would stay out a bit late, she never failed to return.

After spending several nights searching and calling for her dear cat, a heartbroken Vivian decided that she had to accept the reality that Tabby had been taken from her by some accident. She only hoped that Tabby's death had been quick and painless.

For the next few nights after she had given up all hope of Tabby's return, Vivian thought she heard her dear pet meowing each night. Hoping against hope, she would get out of bed and run to the front door, praying that Tabby had come home. But there was no Tabby sheepishly awaiting her on the front porch. Vivian would call out into the darkness and wait for an answering call. Feeling pained ever deeper by her loss, she would close the door and go back to bed, believing that she had only imagined Tabby's familiar cries.

One afternoon, six weeks later, Vivian was pushing the snow off her wooden deck when she again thought she heard Tabby meowing from somewhere close by. She set the snow shovel aside and bent down toward the rough planking of the porch.

This time the meow was fainter in volume, but unmistakable in tone. It was Tabby! At last it occurred to Vivian that her beloved cat had been sealed up in the woodchuck burrow for six weeks.

Within minutes, Vivian had a crew in her backyard, and they were ripping the boards apart with chain saws and wrecking bars. Tabby was lifted out by one of the workmen, who tenderly handed her to Vivian.

Vivian could not hold back her tears. Her dear cat was nothing but fur and bones, but Tabby was alive. Vivian cradled Tabby in her arms and one of the men rushed them to a veterinarian.

After his examination of the emaciated cat, the veterinarian said solemnly that Tabby was scratching at death's door. The veterinarian went on to theorize that the only way Tabby could have survived for six weeks trapped under the deck was if she had managed to find a little water to drink and a few moles to eat. Vivian had rescued her Tabby in the very nick of time.

Amazingly, according to the June 25, 2004, *Daily Record* of London, Bubbles the cat survived for eight weeks trapped under a garden deck, just like Tabby did. Emma Dearie, Bubbles' seven-year-old owner, had continued her desperate search for the kitty for two months and had even walked to farms two miles away to inquire about her beloved pet.

The Dearies' neighbors, John and Anne McMillan, had no idea that they had sealed poor Bubbles in a makeshift kind of tomb when they installed their garden deck. When they at last heard a faint mewing issuing from under the deck, they called a carpenter to pry up a portion. There, they found a very thin and very desperate Bubbles, very glad that someone finally had paid some attention to her cries.

Sara Dearie suggested that the resourceful cat had managed to survive by drinking rainwater and eating insects. Bubbles was placed on a regimen of six meals a day to get her back in shape, and Sara was happy to get her kitty back.

We cannot find any record of anyone claiming that dogs have more than one life, but there is no question that canines have remarkable powers of endurance.

In October, 2004, James Frew of Orphington, Kent, U.K., was walking with his family and their German Spitz Max along the cliffs near Charmouth, Dorset. Max suddenly ran after a blackbird and chased it over the edge of a cliff.

The little blackbird had wings and could easily out-distance Max and soar high above the sea. Max did not have wings, so when he no longer had solid earth beneath him, he plummeted 300 feet to the ground below.

Members of the coast guard helped retrieve Max and expressed their amazement that the dog was simply sitting calmly on the beach awaiting their arrival. He appeared completely unhurt in spite of the great distance he had fallen.

A local dog expert explained that when a dog experiences a sudden, unexpected fall—such as Max's—the dog is unaware of the danger—it's in and its relaxed muscles can prevent serious injury.

Flossy, a sheepdog from Gilleleje, Denmark, was found alive after sixty-eight days trapped in a dry well.

Flossy's owners, Birgitte Pontoppidan and Hans Ibsen, searched for days after their sheepdog went missing, but they had long since given up hope that she would ever return. When Flossie was discovered on August 12, 2003, she had to be lifted out by fire rescue workers.

A local veterinarian theorized that Flossy had only been able to survive by licking condensation off the well walls. She had had no food at all for over two months.

Birgitte and Hans set about restoring Flossy to health with meals of chicken and salmon. To demonstrate their love for the remarkable sheepdog, the couple also pampered her with warm baths. Flossie made a full recovery.

When Georgia, a four-year-old German shepherd, was reunited with her family in March 2004, she was tired, bedraggled, and missing one leg. For three weeks, Georgia had been lost in Marin County, California, and her human family thought they would never see her again.

Georgia disappeared on Valentine's weekend. Guy and Lori Piombo, along with their three sons—Tony, fifteen, and twelve-year-old twins, Vincent and Mario—had been camping at Lawson Landing at Dillon Beach, about seven miles off Highway 1. A camper at a different campsite brought fireworks to the campground, and when he exploded some of them, Georgia, frightened of loud noises, took off running.

The Piombo family spent the rest of the weekend searching for Georgia. They walked the beach, the rolling hills, and the streets of Dillon Beach, searching everywhere for their dog. On Sunday evening, they made the difficult decision to return to Napa without their beloved Georgia.

The next weekend, the Piombos headed back to Lawson Landing, armed with flyers imprinted with Georgia's picture and a full description of the missing German shepherd. Wherever the family went with their flyers and the story of their lost dog, sympathetic individuals volunteered to join the search for Georgia. But once again the weekend came to a close without anyone seeing any sign of the dog. The Piombos sadly drove back to Napa without their dog.

On March 11, a park ranger called the Piombos to report that he had seen a dog matching Georgia's description wandering in the protected wilderness of Point Reyes Seashore. According to the ranger, the dog appeared to be injured and was limping badly as it was slowly making its way on the peninsula, which lay on the opposite side of Tomales Bay from Dillon Beach.

Guy and Mario Piombo loaded a canoe on their pickup truck and headed for Point Reyes National Seashore. They reasoned that in order for Georgia to have reached that particular spot on the peninsula where she had been seen by the park ranger, the dog would have to have walked about seventeen miles along the coast, or it was possible she swam half a mile across the water between the beach and the peninsula.

When the Piombos arrived at the coast, their hopes of finding Georgia were dashed by the heavy winds and high waves that made it impossible to take the canoe out. The next day they managed to sight Georgia with their binoculars, but she was too far away to hear their desperate shouts.

On March 13, it was Vincent's turn to accompany his father to the beach to try to find Georgia and bring her home. The water was calmer that day, and they were able to cross to the beach, where they discovered a series of prints made by a dog with three paws—it seemed that Georgia had injured one of her legs.

Just when it felt as though they were walking in circles following the prints, a park ranger approached the Piombos and informed them that a hiker had found Georgia earlier that day and had called the ranger station. Georgia was safe—she was drinking water and eating cheese at the station.

When Guy and Vincent were reunited with Georgia, the German shepherd wagged her tail for joy, but was unable to jump around because of a missing paw and an injured leg. Guy hoisted Georgia to his shoulders, and father and son hiked the two miles to their canoe with their beloved pet once again a part of the family.

At the veterinarian's office, the decision was made to remove the remainder of Georgia's leg. Dr. Andy Irving of the Lincoln Avenue Pet Hospital told writer Marsha Dorgan of the *Napa Valley Register* (March 19, 2004) that because of the jagged appearance of the cut on Georgia's leg, he thought that a shark had attacked the dog. Dr. Irving also commented that the saga of Georgia was the most unusual and the strangest survival case that he had ever seen.

"To think that [Georgia] ran away, got lost, went for a swim, was attacked by a shark and still was able to swim to land," he said. "How did she even know there was land in that direction? If you asked me what the odds are of survival on this, it would be difficult to calculate."

*R*ena told us of an encounter with the spirits that dwell in the Coconino Forest and the White Mountains near Flagstaff, Arizona. She had this experience as a youngster of twelve when she visited her grandparents with her nine-year-old brother, Lloyd.

"Lloyd and I always loved the two weeks in the summer that we spent with Grandpa and Grandma Reyes in their beautiful old ranch style home outside of Flagstaff," Rena said. "Of course, we saw them other times of the year, but always with Mom and Dad. During these two weeks, we had Grandpa and Grandma all to ourselves. Sometime during our stay, we would always visit the Lowell Observatory and see the stars or maybe drive up to tour the Grand Canyon."

Back in the early 1960s, Flagstaff was far less developed than it is today, and there were many places not so very far from downtown for people to go hiking, picnicking, and camping.

One very warm day in July, their grandparents took Rena and Lloyd for a long hike through the woods and then returned to the ranch house. Although Rena and Lloyd complained about being hot, they knew their parents were sweltering in Phoenix, where it was supposed to reach 120-degrees that day.

"Grandma had set out on the patio four potatoes for baking in the fire pit," Rena recalled, but when we went out to start the charcoal, we found that someone had left four rocks in the place of the four potatoes."

While they were puzzling over the mysterious disappearance of the potatoes, Lloyd came running out to the patio from his room, shouting that someone had taken his new harmonica. Since Rena had complained about how terrible he sounded when he was learning how to play it, Lloyd immediately suspected that his sister had hidden it.

"Grandpa had planned on taking a nap before dinner," Rena said, "but he came out to the patio, kind of grouchy, and asked what all the commotion was about."

Grandma explained the disappearance of the potatoes while Lloyd accused Rena of hiding his harmonica and leaving a pinecone in its place.

"Grandpa suddenly got very serious," Rena said, "and kind of narrowed his eyes, the same way he did when he told us ghost stories around the fire pit at night. Then he asked me if I had made a prayer to the spirits of the forest before our hike."

Rena remembered answering that she didn't know she was supposed to pray to any spirits or she certainly would have done so.

Grandpa merely arched an eyebrow and sniffed. Then turning to Lloyd, he asked the child if he had asked permission of the spirits of old that had walked the trails for many generations whether Lloyd and Rena might enter the forest.

Lloyd turned pale and shook his head. If he had known . . .

Grandpa told them that he thought it was understood that respect must be paid to the spirits of the Navajo and the Apache who loved these mountains and forests and to the Old Ones who had built the ruins that now lay outside of Flagstaff and Sedona. Since they had not given proper respect to the beings that had once walked the sacred places, the spirits had come into the Reyes' home and had taken things to appease them.

"That was when Grandma spoke up and scolded Grandpa for scaring us kids with ghost talk," Rena said. "She said that there were little spooks walking around, all right, but they were furry little spirits that were very much alive. And they would very likely return."

Grandpa laughed and admitted that these ghosts were very visible and very active—and he told Rena and Lloyd that since the spooks had apparently already come and gone twice that afternoon while the family was hiking, they would very likely come back again before dark.

He told the grandkids to follow him to the bushes beside the ranch house. While they stayed behind the bushes, he walked out to a clearing and placed a shiny new penny on a flat stone.

"Grandpa joined Lloyd and me behind the bushes and indicated that we should be quiet," Rena said. "I remember that sweat was running down my back in rivulets, and I was wondering if this was another of Grandpa's jokes. If it was, I was just too hot and tired to enjoy it. It seemed we crouched in those bushes for hours—although it was probably fifteen minutes at the most—when Grandpa suddenly pointed toward a small, brown furry creature creeping up to the penny."

The little animal seized the coin and scurried off into the trees. Lloyd squealed his surprise: "That rat stole your penny, Grandpa!"

"Ah, but just wait," Grandpa said. "You see, he's not really a thief, he's a trader. An honest trader, at that. He'll come back in a little while and give me something in return for my penny."

Rena and Lloyd were still puzzling over Grandpa's words when the rat was back at the flat rock in the clearing, and they could see that it bore something in its teeth. Without further ceremony, the rat placed a bit of shiny glass where the penny had been.

"So that's your ghost," Grandpa chuckled. "Some people call them wood rats, pack rats, or trading rats. Sometimes we get a nest of them around here, and I guess we have us another one now. If we find the nest, we'll find Grandma's potatoes and Lloyd's harmonica."

Rena recalled a discussion in Miss Gonzalez's class that spring. "Trade rats," she echoed. "I remember, they take something from someone and always leave something in return."

"Well, not always," Grandpa chuckled. "But usually. Most often they trade for something to use in building their nests. But they do love bright, shiny objects. That's why Lloyd's new silver harmonica appealed to one of them."

Rena couldn't suppress a shiver. "They're kind of cute, Grandpa," she allowed, "but are we really going to let them run around in the house?"

Grandpa laughed and said they would decline that pleasure. "Now that we know there is an active nest near us, we'll be more careful about closing doors."

The three of them followed the trade rat to its nest. Grandpa was correct. It wasn't far from the ranch house, and it was built of branches, twigs, sticks, and other debris. Located at the base of a tree and extending several feet to a rocky ledge, the nest's construction reminded Rena of a beaver dam.

"Grandpa shooed a couple rats away from the nest while he reached in and grabbed Lloyd's harmonica," Rena recalled. "They didn't seem particularly vicious, but they were about fifteen inches in length, including their long tails, and there was no way that I would've stuck my hand in there. To heck with Lloyd's harmonica!"

Grandpa handed Lloyd his prized musical instrument and shrugged his shoulders about the fate of Grandma's potatoes. "We'll let the rats keep the potatoes," he smiled. "She has a whole bag full."

As they were walking away from the nest, Lloyd stopped and turned back. He took a nickel from his pocket and placed it in the rats' nest.

"I want to be an honest trader, too," he said. "Grandpa took back my harmonica for me, so I'm giving the trader rats a nickel in return."

Rena said that she had never loved her brother more than at that moment. But she didn't let him put the harmonica in his mouth until it had undergone an extensive sterilization process.

"For the rest of those two weeks, we played traders with those remarkable little wood rats," Rena said. "Every day, we would go out to the flat rock in the clearing and leave a pretty stone, a bit of glass, one of my jumping jacks. And within an hour or so, the rats would take it and later return a trade item, such as a pinecone, a stick, or a pebble.

"We did go to the Lowell Observatory and look at the stars and marvel in our kids' minds about the wonder of the universe," Rena concluded, "but the wonder and beauty of Mother Nature has never been expressed better to my way of thinking than the summer when Lloyd and I interacted with those trade rats. Never before had I respected the intelligence and the intricacies to be found in a nonhuman environment and social order. Those were some powerful lessons that Lloyd and I learned from those industrious, honest trade rats."

*O*f all the many categories of pet miracles, some of the most amazing are the sagas of animals that find their way back home after having been lost. Perhaps even more remarkable than those, however, are the accounts of pets that somehow divine their way to their owners' new homes even though the pets have never been to the new homes.

In *Dog Miracles*, we told the unforgettable story of Bobbie, "the great collie of Oregon," who in 1923 accomplished an extraordinary odyssey of 3,000 miles from Wolcott, Indiana, where his owner had been visiting relatives, back to his home in Silverston, Oregon. Crossing a wide variety of inhospitable terrains and suffering numerous injuries, Bobbie managed to arrive home after six months of steady walking.

The stalwart collie's incredible journey was nearly equaled by a cat named Tom, who in 1949 trekked a bit over 2,500 miles from St. Petersburg, Florida, to San Gabriel, California, to be reunited with Mr. and Mrs. Charles B. Smith. The Smiths had left him behind because they were concerned that Tom wouldn't adjust to driving such a long distance in an automobile. It took Tom two years and six weeks to find his owners' new home, but bear in mind he had to find a place where he had never been! Tom managed to locate a completely new residence in a state on the opposite coast. Such a feat truly qualifies as a pet miracle.

Li-Ping, a big, black cat, was left behind when owner Vivian Allgood, a registered nurse, accepted employment in Orlando in April 1955. She thought it was best to leave her beloved Li-Ping with her sister in Sandusky, Ohio.

In May, about a month after her move, Vivian was sitting outside on a porch talking with a friend when she noticed a sorry-looking, scratched, and half-furless cat limping its way toward her. She could scarcely believe her eyes, but she recognized Li-Ping. Large hunks of

Pet Miracles

hair had been torn from his body in what must have been innumerable fights to the finish. His feet were raw and bleeding from averaging about fifty-three miles a day to complete the 1,586-mile hike. After he found his way to Florida, each day for a week Vivian Allgood provided Li-Ping with his fill of milk and liver until his many wounds and his sore feet finally healed.

How Li-Ping found his way from Ohio to Florida and how Tom made his incredible trek from Florida to California—destinations beyond their possible experience or knowledge—cannot be explained. Li-Ping had never been to Orlando; Tom had never before traveled to California. In each case, the cat had no awareness about where the owners had moved. Even if Tom had heard Mrs. and Mr. Smith speaking about "San Gabriel" and Li-Ping had overheard "Orlando," what would such words mean to a cat? And it is beyond reasonable imagination to visualize a cat walking down the highway with a road map tucked under its chin, thumbing a paw for a ride.

While we're on the topic of mysterious reunions, there could be few stranger than the one enjoyed by U.S. Army Captain Stanley C. Raye and Joker, in which the cocker spaniel found his way from a town in California to a Pacific island military base thousands of miles away.

When Captain Raye received his orders for overseas duty in the South Pacific during World War II, he had no choice other than to leave Joker with friends in Pittsburg, California. The cocker spaniel was oblivious to news of the war and to the reasons why his beloved owner would leave him. Joker only knew that Raye had left him and that he was feeling plain miserable about the circumstances. Joker spent two weeks in what seemed to be a state of depression, and then, suddenly, he seemed to have a plan.

Joker ran away from his foster home in Pittsburg and headed for Oakland, about thirty miles away. Later, once the remarkable story was pieced together, two army doctors remembered seeing a stray cocker spaniel hanging around the dock area.

Through a process of selection that cannot be defined by any present-day scholar, Joker chose one particular army transport upon which to stow away. When he was discovered well out to sea, an officer ordered Joker destroyed. This saga would have ended with Joker becoming shark food had it not been for a sympathetic army major who volunteered to adopt the wayward pup.

The transport made several ports of call in the Pacific, and at each docking, Joker was at the helm, sniffing the air and appearing to study the seaport. When the ship docked at one particular island, Joker jumped ship and raced ashore, his frantic adoptive owner in close pursuit.

With the major who accepted responsibility for Joker and several enlisted men running after him, the cocker spaniel didn't stop running until he was barking joyfully and jumping around the feet of an overwhelmed Captain Raye. Although the major had become very fond of Joker, he could not dispute the dog's obvious elation at his reunion with the captain. It was apparent to all observers that the courageous cocker spaniel had found his true master.

How Joker had managed to track Captain Raye from his home in California to a faraway island in the South Pacific presents an almost unfathomable mystery. All the cocker spaniel knew for certain was that his devoted master had left him. It is inconceivable that Joker could have comprehended the concept that "military orders" had taken Captain Raye away from him. It is doubtful that the captain himself knew his particular destination until he arrived there, but what would the name of a Pacific island have meant to a cocker spaniel in California if the captain had mentioned the location of the military base to friends? With the strict "a slip of a lip can sink a ship" policy of secrecy concerning military maneuvers and projects that was enforced during World War II, it is highly unlikely that Captain Raye would have shared such information with friends even if he had known the place of his deployment in advance.

On January 20, 1958, nearly thirteen years after the unconditional surrender of Japan on August 14, 1945, and the end of the conflict in the Pacific, the Associated Press did a follow-up story on Captain Raye and Joker. The two had remained inseparable until Joker's death earlier that month in Great Falls, Montana. The remarkable cocker spaniel had lived a full and rich fourteen and one-half years.

Joker took his secrets with him to his grave. However, even if the cocker spaniel had been gifted with intelligent vocalization, could he really have explained what unseen force had led him to the Oakland port so that he might stow away aboard a vessel that would take him to his owner? Could he really have articulated what greater intelligence told him precisely which island was harboring his master among the many ports of call at which the transport stopped? Quite likely not. Joker's remarkable reunion with his master Captain Stanley C. Raye may perhaps forever remain in the file of unsolved mysteries and astonishing pet miracles.

ow we will leave the subject of mysterious reunions to present some additional odysseys that are quite miraculous. But these are due to the more understandable traits of courage, strength, perseverance, determination, and endurance.

In 1979, Nick, a German shepherd, became separated from her owner, Doug Simpson, during a camping trip in the southern Arizona desert. Four months later, Nick staggered back to her home in Selah, Washington. Somehow, assuming that Nick was able to walk a more or less straight line from Arizona to Washington, she managed to walk through some of the roughest country on earth, terrain that included the Grand Canyon, a number of icy rivers, and the towering, snow-covered mountains of Nevada and Oregon.

In 1986, when his owner, Linda Thompson, decided to leave Beaver Dam, Wisconsin, to test the climate in Tucson, Arizona, Sam the Siamese cat moved along with her. After about a year, however, Linda decided that she preferred the climate in Wisconsin, and she made plans to return. Trouble arose when her new landlords in Beaver Dam said that Sam would not be welcome: absolutely no pets allowed. Linda bade a sad farewell to her friend Sam and put him up for adoption at the Humane Society in Tucson.

In 1991, some of Linda's friends from her former neighborhood in Beaver Dam called her and said that she had better come and check out the ornery, frazzled cat haunting the place. Although it seemed impossible, she was astonished to see that Sam had managed to wend the 1,400 miles back to Wisconsin from Arizona.

There are certain instances when a cat gets homesick for a former residence and decides to return to a familiar place—whether its owners care to come or not.

✿ ❂ ✿   *Pet Miracles*   ✿ ❂ ✿

In April 1996, the Todd family moved from Farmington, Utah, to Seattle, Washington. Although the Todds liked their new environment just fine, Ninja, their cat, decided that he preferred the mouse hunting in Utah. Within a few days after the family's arrival in Seattle, Ninja jumped over the fence and began his trek back through 850 miles of treacherous rivers, rugged mountains, and dense forests.

About a year later, the Todds' former neighbors in Farmington were awakened in the middle of the night by a distinctive—and once very familiar—caterwaul. Although at first they couldn't believe their ears, in the full light of the dawn, they discovered Ninja at their back door.

The neighbors, the Parker family, called the Todds and offered to ship Ninja back to them in Seattle, but after a brief family council, the Todds voted to allow Ninja to remain in the place that he loved the best—with the Parkers.

In February 2004, Ms. Zhu, of Beijing, China, gave one of her cats away to a friend because she was uncomfortable with the animal's poor hygiene. Although the friend protested that it was obvious the cat loved Zhu, she was adamant. She had owned the cat for three years, she stated, and it simply did not clean itself as meticulously as the others.

However, forty days later, the rejected cat found its way back to Zhu from the friend's home—more than sixty miles away.

Zhu softened her heart. It was apparent that the cat loved her and was homesick for her. And it was also very apparent that the cat had suffered a great deal to accomplish the return to its home. On March 4, 2004, the *China Daily* quoted Ms. Zhu's comment to the *Beijing Times* that the cat who had once weighed nearly five pounds had returned to her weighing only a little more than a pound. Ms. Zhu added that she would never again send the cat away.

Somehow, while staying in a Sacramento, California, motel in 1961, Joe Martinez became separated from Chinook, his beloved white German shepherd. Although he spent hours searching, Martinez was forced to accept the sad fact that his dog had vanished.

In March 1964, three years after he had gone missing, Chinook limped, weary and ragged, into the yard of Martinez's home in Scottsbluff, Nebraska. It had taken the brave shepherd three years to make the 1,400 journey from Sacramento to Scottsbluff.

In 1992, Paquita Soler of Gandia, Spain, was advised to travel to Paris for medical treatment and to be prepared to remain in France for at least two months. She was relieved when some friends who lived in the French town of Montpellier offered to board Lord, her beloved canine companion, for the duration of her treatment.

Though the medical treatment was successful, Paquita's peace of mind was demolished when she returned to her friends' home in January 1993 and was sadly informed that Lord had run away. He had been so grieved by Paquita's absence that he left one night and had not been seen for weeks. Paquita was heartbroken to imagine that Lord was wandering about in a confused state of mind in south central France, more than 500 miles from their home in Spain.

And then one day in June 1993, Paquita was overjoyed to hear a familiar scratching at the door. A bedraggled, scruffy, bleeding Lord was asking to be let in. Miraculously, Lord had made his way home to southeastern Spain from Montpellier, France—a distance of more than 500 miles. For five months, he had worked his way across mountains, through forests, and around dangerous highways to be reunited with his mistress.

In April 2004, Floridian Pamela Edwards received a call from the local animal shelter telling her that Cheyenne, her cat, had been found—over 3,000 miles away—in San Francisco.

Ms. Edwards was taken momentarily off guard. She had once owned a black, shorthaired cat named Cheyenne, that was true. But the feline walked out the door in November 1997 and had never returned.

It couldn't be her cat, she told the shelter. She had never lived in San Francisco. How could Cheyenne have walked out a door in Florida and arrived in a city on the West coast?

But the evidence was conclusive: The black, short-haired cat in San Francisco who was awaiting a reunion with its owner was really Cheyenne. When Pamela Edwards had adopted Cheyenne from her local animal shelter, she had the cat implanted with a microchip. Cheyenne had been a healthy three-year-old female, and Pamela wanted to guard against the possibility of the cat straying or being stolen. When Pamela understood that the reason she had been called was because of the microchip in the cat's skin, Pamela joyfully accepted the news that Cheyenne had been found after a seven-year absence.

After Pamela had been reunited with her now ten-year-old cat, Deb Campbell, of Animal Care and Control in San Francisco, theorized that someone had found Cheyenne wandering the streets of the city and dropped her off with a staff member.

How had Cheyenne materialized in San Francisco in the first place?

The statutes of limitation for catnapping had probably elapsed, but suspicions pointed toward a former neighbor who admired the black cat and who had moved to San Francisco around the same time Cheyenne disappeared.

When staff nurse Adria Bryan was driving to work in Rhyl, North Wales, on the morning of May 20, 2004, she soon became aware that many oncoming motorists were flashing their lights at her. At first she thought maybe she was driving a bit too fast at sixty miles per hour, but then she passed a police car, and the officer didn't turn on either the warning lights or siren.

Finally, a young man pulled alongside her and pointed to the roof of her car. "It must be my purse!" she thought. Perhaps she had left her purse on the roof of her car as she was getting in the driver's seat that morning? No. Her purse was securely positioned on the seat beside her.

At last, completely perplexed as to why she was the object of so many motorists' attention and flashing lights, she pulled her Ford Escort over to the side of the road and got out.

There, still clinging on for dear life to the groove at the top of the rear door, was Joe, her cat.

A trifle wind-blown, Joe seemed grateful to be lifted into the car by his owner, but he didn't overplay the whole gratitude thing. After all, he had managed to hang onto the roof for at least four miles at high speeds and still keep his cool.

Either Joe exhibited a little too much confidence or felt his proverbial nine lives would stand him in good stead, for a couple of days later, he got into a fight with a bull terrier. Once again Joe survived—but he suffered three cracked ribs and a punctured lung.

When John Sutton of Tauranga, New Zealand, got pulled over by the flashing lights of an unmarked police car while he was driving to work on April 2, 2004, he could not imagine what he had done to run afoul of the law.

As he slowed his Toyota Celica and pulled over to the side of the highway, he was startled to see Bono, his grey Persian, slide down the windshield and grip the wipers with his claws. Although Sutton thought that he had chased Bono away from the car before leaving for work, the rascal had quite obviously jumped back up on the roof as Sutton was backing out of the driveway.

The patrol officer was quite surprised to see a real cat sprawled across the windshield. He had pulled Sutton over because he thought Bono was a fluffy toy or stuffed cat that had been placed on the roof as a joke.

Bono was clearly shaken by the ordeal, and John Sutton said he hoped the cat had learned a lesson. John learned a lesson—he always checks his roof before he gets in the car to drive to work!

Our longtime friend and colleague, Bill Wundram, of the *Quad-City Times* in Davenport, Iowa, has written about the seemingly supernatural sense of a tiger cat named Sissy Cat who appears to know when a patient at Ridgecrest Village is near death. Pat Oostendorp, activity director of the nursing center, told Wundrum that she had tracked a dozen cases in which Sissy Cat had come into a patient's room and stayed there until the person's death. For days and days, Pat said, the psychic cat will climb onto the patient's bed or sit in the chair with him or her, offering comfort and affection, until the patient passes.

Becky Blumer, director of nursing at Ridgecrest Village, agreed with Pat, asserting that Sissy Cat had an uncanny sense that bordered on the supernatural.

Sissy Cat came to Ridgecrest in 2000 and immediately made herself at home in the nursing center, which has 100 beds and is home to critically ill patients. From the very beginning of her tenure at the center, Sissy Cat seemed most interested in visiting those who were about to die. Many patients and their families remarked that Sissy Cat appeared to comfort and care for them as if she were "half human."

In one instance, Leonard, an eighty-five-year-old man, came to the nursing wing, and Sissy Cat immediately entered his room to take a position at the foot of his bed. When Leonard was in pain, Sissy Cat stroked his arm with a paw. Leonard's wife said that they had never had a cat in their sixty-two years of marriage, but her husband and Sissy Cat experienced an immediate bonding. Several days later, after Leonard had passed away, Sissy Cat climbed onto his empty bed, then jumped to the floor and walked around the bed two times. When she was told that Leonard had died, Sissy Cat left the room.

Pat Oostendorp told Wundrum that it often seemed as though God had sent Sissy Cat down to comfort those on the edge of death. "One has to see it to believe it, the way she immediately attaches herself to those who are about to die," the activity director said. "She's like an angel."

Although Ms. Oostendorp conceded that such statements might seem odd to some people, she had seen Sissy Cat attach herself to too many terminally ill patients not to know "that something is uncanny, extrasensory about her."

Some years ago, we learned of Inky, a jet-black, ten-pound Chihuahua-mixed breed, who had been trained for medical duties. For many years, Inky made three healing rounds daily at the fifty-bed Hospice of St. John in Lakewood, Colorado. With an uncanny instinct that directed her to the beds of those terminally ill patients who needed her most, Inky accomplished some of the most impressive emotional healing that the nurses at the hospice had ever witnessed. Staff members noted how Inky had a remarkable ability to ascertain the needs of the patients. For those who really needed her, Inky would spend the entire night. If there were two patients who needed her, Inky somehow intuitively and painstakingly divided her time between them.

Pam Currier, a former director of the hospice, once told a reporter that in many instances Inky was more effective than a human therapist. Ms. Currier explained that to the lonely patient, Inky could be a friend; to the depressed patient, a clown; and to the anxious patient, a diversion.

Patients who had been on the receiving end of care for many months could find in Inky someone to cherish.

Hospice personnel have long been saddened by the number of patients who die without loved ones by their side. For such men and women, the perky presence of a dog or cat can be a true blessing.

Nursing director Rose Griffith stated that Inky brought life and humor back to the terminally ill, those whose existence has been dulled by pain, fear, and loneliness.

Sister Helen Reynolds, of the Sisters of Loretto, is credited for the acquisition and training of canine therapists who work with the dying. Sister Helen wanted to find dogs that would not hesitate to jump into people's laps and to spread love impartially. She found such an animal in Inky, who had been awaiting her own death sentence in an animal shelter.

One of the directors of the hospice said that she would never know how many patients died easier, how many grieving families were consoled, how many nurses were strengthened to carry on—all because of a bundle of love named Inky.

When we lived in Scottsdale, Arizona, we were made aware of Buddy, a mixed-breed mutt, who was (like Inky) saved from death row in a dog pound to brighten the life of gravely ill patients. Robin Tenny, director of the cancer unit at Desert Samaritan Hospital in Mesa, Arizona, said that Buddy worked wonders when he visited patients wearing such colorful costumes as Uncle Sam, complete with top hat and a stars-and-stripes neckerchief.

Rescued from death by Robin and her husband, John, Buddy had to pass rigorous tests before becoming qualified to join the elite ranks of 8,000 registered therapy dogs in the United States. Paula Cingota, head of the San Diego chapter of Therapy Dogs International, certified Buddy as Arizona's first therapy dog in the fall of 1991.

Robin Tenny commented that the patients suffering from terminal cancer were always in great pain—but they glowed when Buddy came around to see them. To all the hospice workers, it was exciting to see smiles on faces that hadn't smiled in days.

everal years ago, Sherry Steiger learned that Ken Bakehouse was no stranger to miracles. He told her that he had experienced many miracles in his life of nearly eighty years, yet it had come as quite a surprise when one of his biggest miracles ever was delivered through one of God's tiniest creatures—a little four-legged pet Pomeranian belonging to the neighbor next door.

A professional photographer by trade, for over forty-five years Ken operated a photography studio out of the building adjoining his home in Washington, Iowa. As fate would have it, the business that he owned, loved, and cherished as his livelihood for so many years would be instrumental in the building's demolition.

Ken told Sherry that he was cozy in his bed on the night of September 30 in a deep, comfortable sleep—totally oblivious to the sudden catastrophe that had broken out. The chemicals he used in processing and developing film had fueled a large fire, and they were empowering its rapid spread. The life-threatening fire was advancing at such a rapid rate that not even the most agile person half as young as Ken would have been capable of escaping without Divine intervention, and it couldn't have come one minute later!

"If it hadn't been for God's little angel, Sam," Ken related to Sherry, "there could have been several of us who might have died in that fire."

Ken's neighbor, Bessie Bell, who was also sound asleep in her bed, had been crudely awakened by the thumps and bumps of her beloved dog, Sam, who was mysteriously misbehaving. Bessie's bed was forbidden territory to Sam—he knew it was the law to not even attempt such a jump, and a jump up onto the bed would be a bit intimidating for such an itsy bitsy dog. Sam had always obeyed—except this time, when he somehow made it up on the bed and was most erratically jumping up and down on his master's body.

Startled and slightly annoyed at this peculiar behavior, Bessie was about to give an intense scolding to Sam for such a rude awakening, but when she sat up in bed to do so, she was stopped by the sight of flames shooting out of Ken Bakehouse's buildings. Ms. Bell frantically dialed 911, and then, realizing how fast the inferno was enveloping everything in sight, she didn't even wait to talk with the dispatcher, but instead grabbed her little Pomeranian pooch and made an escape outside. "Let's get out of here, we're not going to burn," she appreciatively said to Sam, realizing he hadn't been naughty after all!

Bessie had not waited to speak with a dispatcher to relay the emergency information and location, but when she thought she was about to fall she managed to push her emergency lifeline button that summoned help. Thanks to that technology, the push of the button registered the address of the incoming call to the sheriff's department, and it didn't take long for a police car and ambulance to arrive at the scene. The fire department was then alerted, making its presence in record time.

At 1:15 a.m., a startled Ken Bakehouse awoke to shouts and screams of, "Hey, your building is on fire!" Although Ken was able to get out of his home without injury, he had barely made it out before the firestorm engulfed everything he owned. His entire studio and all his equipment were burned up in what seemed like minutes.

One can imagine the mixed emotions Ken was experiencing with the gratitude of being rescued unharmed, yet the grief of knowing his business and home were obliterated and there was no insurance to cover the damage and losses. Ken had been forced to drop his insurance because the premiums to insure his photography equipment and supplies had continued to rise to such a cost that he couldn't maintain it.

In telling Sherry about how deeply grateful he was at the mystery and wonder of a dog sensing the fire and being instrumental to saving Bessie Bell's life and his own, Ken was not shy at giving the entire praise to the miracle working power of God. To Sherry, the miracle extended beyond the heroic rescue by Bessie's pet, Sam, and attested to Ken's spirit and faith.

Ken had experienced trial by fire in tragedies and calamities of the heart just before this particular episode. Within a short period of time, Ken's wife suffered a stroke that left her in need of full-time assistance in a care center. Shortly thereafter, his daughter was diagnosed with cancer. It would be easy for the best of us to feel down and in despair, even in being spared from physical harm in the fire. Who among us would blame Ken for thinking, "Why me, Lord?" but his strength of character and belief are an example to behold.

"I could have been seriously burned, or worse, died," Ken said. Continuing, he added, "I'm so grateful that even though I have lost everything, I have my life, and I'm not going to let the devil steal my joy! The things I lost are only material."

This sentiment would have been freshly on Ken's mind, for in what seems like an amazingly cruel and unfair irony to Ken's staggering losses, only several days before the fire, he had witnessed firsthand how the ravages of such a blaze had affected the life of a wonderful woman and changed her life forever.

Ken had recently helped Christie Humphries set up for a concert after a very long absence from her profession as an accomplished pianist. Her life had been brutally interrupted by a fire that left her very seriously injured. Christie had been through a long period of painful rehabilitation, suffering burns on over 85 percent of her body. Left with only five fingers between both of her hands to play the piano, she triumphantly endured the strenuous process toward comeback and Ken, admiring her fortitude, was eager to help her in any way possible.

Realizing that he could have been in that position himself, he again praised the wonder of that little dog next door. "With what Christie went through with the agony of burns and suffering, what have I got to complain about?" he said.

Ken keeps a positive attitude. Even though his career was wiped out by the loss of all his equipment and studio, he told Sherry he had been keeping himself busy by writing songs. In spite of trials, Ken managed to write words and music to nearly 100 inspirational songs that he hoped might be uplifting to others going through tough times. He was using a portable piano keyboard to back himself up and he still sang the praises as well to good neighbor Sam, the Pomeranian!

❖ ❖ ❖   *Pet Miracles*   ❖ ❖ ❖

*P*atrolman John Bassler, an assistant trainer in Pittsburgh K-9 school, didn't give it a second thought before he used the "kiss of life," mouth-to-mouth resuscitation, to save his dog Heidi's life.

Heidi had come running toward him with a tennis ball lodged in her throat. By the time he removed the object, his beloved pet had stopped breathing. Her eyes were glazed over, and her tongue was extended, swollen, and purplish in color. He could detect no heartbeat.

Bassler held Heidi's mouth shut, put his mouth over her nose, and then gave her three good breaths. He felt Heidi's chest rise and expand. He knelt beside her and gave her three chest compressions. Then he saw her eyes blink, and in a couple of minutes she was fine.

Do you love your dog enough to give it the kiss of life should it stop breathing? What about your cat? Surely, you are probably thinking, I love old Fido or Felix enough to get down on my knees, hold his mouth shut, put my mouth over his nose, and give him three good breaths.

We don't doubt that your intentions are good and that you would do whatever you could to try to save your beloved pet. You would even administer the kiss of life, the very breath of existence.

But what if your pet was a rattlesnake?

Zookeeper Mark O'Shea continued to breathe into the throat of a deadly diamondback rattler for five and a half hours before he had restored it to life.

O'Shea, an expert on snakes for a popular safari park in England, was horrified to discover the rattlesnake being swallowed by its cage mate, a giant California king snake. The zookeeper yanked the half-swallowed rattler free from the jaws of the king snake, but found that its heart had stopped.

O'Shea didn't actually place his mouth over the rattler's, but he did slide a tube down the snake's throat and began practicing the breath of life. It took him nearly six hours of steady effort, but his dogged persistence was rewarded when he at last brought the rattler back to consciousness.

The exhausted but delighted O'Shea named the rattlesnake Lazarus and saw to it that from that time on it had a cage of its own.

When seventy-three-year-old Ed Crossan died in January 2004, Polo, his three-year-old Labrador and German shepherd mix, got to his feet and ran out of the house in the Philadelphia suburb. Calls to summon the dog back home were unsuccessful, so members of the family went to look for the grief-stricken dog.

After searching the neighborhood and streets beyond, they couldn't find their father's beloved friend anywhere. Ed's daughter Donna said that they wanted to spend more time searching for Polo, but they had to go to the funeral home to make the arrangements for their father.

To the astonishment of the entire family, the family later sighted Polo pacing back and forth in front of the Wade Funeral home, about a mile away. Ed's other daughter, Theresa, told the Bucks County Courier that they couldn't believe that the dog had somehow known where his master would be taken and had arrived there before the family did.

The next day, Polo disappeared again, but this time the Crossans knew where to look. Once again, they found him pacing restlessly in front of the funeral home.

Accounts such as Polo's, of a faithful dog's undying devotion to an owner, are not uncommon.

When Mario Allegritti died in February 1989, his dog, Diana, ran away after the funeral service. His sons searched for her off and on for a few days, and ultimately decided that she had gone away for good.

Fourteen months later, as Mrs. Allegritti stopped by the cemetery to visit her husband's grave, she was surprised to see the caretaker trying to chase a dog away from the tombstone. Although the animal was starved and bedraggled, Mrs. Allegritti recognized the dog as Diana. According to the caretaker, the dog had come to the grave every night.

Mrs. Allegritti informed the astonished man that the dog had belonged to her husband. The widow tried to pick the dog up in her arms, but Diana wriggled free and began to whine. Once unrestrained, Diana went directly to Mario's tombstone and licked the picture that had been set in a cameo atop the gravestone. After Diana had performed that little ritual, she seemed willing to accompany her master's wife back to the car.

From that evening on, until Diana died in the mid-1990s, either Mrs. Allegritti or one of her sons would accompany the dog to the cemetery. While they observed, Diana would walk directly to Mario's tombstone, lick his picture, and then crouch in front of the grave, not once taking her eyes from her master's likeness.

In 1992, fifty years after the death of Shep, a collie–German shepherd mix, the people of Fort Benton, Montana, held a grand ceremony at his monument to honor the memory of a dog's loyalty and devotion.

In 1936, Roy Castles, a sheepherder and Shep's owner, felt very sick and went to the hospital in Fort Benton. A few days later, Roy passed away, and attendants carried him out of the place in a wooden box.

Shep became very confused when Roy died. Old Roy had been his inseparable companion, and the two of them had spent night after night, month after month, alone with the sheep herds. Now Ray wouldn't speak to him, wouldn't pet him. He was stone cold and in a box.

Some men loaded Ray aboard a Great Northern train headed east, and Shep was left all alone, whining and confused. He stayed there on the platform and watched the trains coming in and leaving. Some folks got on, others got off. Perhaps Ray would be coming back soon.

In those days, Fort Benton received four daily incoming trains. Shep was there the next day to meet all four. When Ray didn't step off any of them, Shep came back the next day...and the next...and the next. The faithful dog maintained his mournful vigil for nearly six years, greeting each train with expectation, and then walking dejectedly away from each disappointment.

The railroad workers didn't run him off. In fact, they developed a healthy respect for such a remarkable display of faithfulness and loyalty—and many of them saw to it that Shep got plenty of scraps to eat. Eventually the collie–German shepherd dug a home under the station's boardwalk so he wouldn't have so far to walk back and forth to check on the train arrivals. Some of the railroad workers brought Shep old blankets to help keep him warm in the cold of winter.

In 1942, at the age of fifteen, Shep slipped under the wheels of one of the trains that he came running to meet, and his six-year vigil came to an end. When some of the railroad workers buried the old dog on the top of a bluff overlooking the tracks, one of them remarked that Shep and Ray were finally together once again.

A finely crafted, life-sized granite statue of a New-foundland dog serves as a grave-marker in the Rock Island, Illinois, Chippiannock Cemetery. In his March 5, 1993, column in the *Quad City Times*, Bill Wundram quoted Greg Vogele, cemetery manager, who told him that the statue was a replica of a devoted Newfound-land who is said to have died of a broken heart. The dog could not go on after the deaths of two children in the 1878 diphtheria epidemic that struck the area. According to old newspaper accounts, the lung disease brought a swift death to five-year-old Eddie and his sister, Josie, eight. One day the big Newfoundland had walked them home as usual—and two days later the children were dead.

The faithful Newfoundland, whose name has been lost to the ages, was completely distraught by the deaths of his little master and mistress. He walked behind the hearse that carried the tiny caskets to the cemetery and returned daily to grieve at their graves. He would walk to the cemetery each morning and lie on their gravesites until dark. Less than a year after the deaths of Eddie and Josie, the big dog, who had often refused food during this time, literally died of sorrow for his little human charges. He was buried on the family acreage.

The children's father, O.J. Dimick, a businessman of considerable wealth, had been so touched by the Newfoundland's devotion he commissioned a Chicago sculptor to create a life-sized replica of the dog that could be placed over the graves of Eddie and Josie. According to contemporary accounts, Dimick's instructions to the sculptor included the comments that the dog's likeness should be the very best quality, with his head resting on his paws in a natural position. Dimick also ensured the statue of the dog should forever watch over the two little ones whose images he so revered.

There are many accounts of a dog's devotion to a deceased master or mistress that we could cite, but it is most unusual to discover such a story concerning a bull.

In March 2004, Barnaby the bull broke the fence of his pasture near the German town of Roedental soon after his owner, Alfred Gruenemeyer, was buried. According to baffled eyewitnesses, Barnaby walked one mile to the cemetery, jumped over a wall, and found his deceased owner's exact cemetery plot. Here he remained for days, resisting all efforts to coax or to drag him away.

At last, after several days of mourning and paying his last respects, Barnaby allowed himself to be led away and was returned to his pasture. Neighbors testified that farmer Gruenemeyer had treated all his animals as pets, and he had even occasionally allowed Barnaby run of his home.

Veterinarians who became acquainted with the strange trek of Barnaby agreed that it was common to learn of dogs that mourned for their late owners, but none of them had ever heard of a bull pining for its lost master. Veterinarian Klaus Mueller commented that Barnaby exhibited a remarkable level of intelligence, but he could offer no explanation how the bull could have found the exact spot where his master was buried.

*J*olinda, nine years old, told us the following story about her favorite pet and the most unusual way she came to discover what she called a miracle.

Jolinda had been sent on a mission—to retrieve her brother, Ricardo, who was very late for dinner. Jolinda didn't have to be psychic to sense the frustration that was building in her mother, with an anxiety that might burst any minute into a lava flow that would scald anything in its path. It was nearing the danger point after twenty minutes of both Mama and Jolinda taking turns dialing the phone number of the home where Ricardo was doing homework with his friend Ron where they repeatedly got only a busy signal.

When the pot of spaghetti on one burner and the pot of sauce on the other both started to boil over on the stove, Jolinda knew she'd better come up with a helpful solution.

"Don't worry, Mom, I'll just go get him. I'll take my bike and be back really fast. You just go if you have to, so you won't be late. We'll be okay," Jolinda urged, as she gave a hug of additional assurance. It was at least five blocks away to Ron's house and her Mom didn't have much time before she had to be at a most important parent/teacher meeting at the school twenty minutes away.

Everything had gone wrong, and Ricardo being forty-five minutes late offered no time to debate the issue. Jolinda caught a slight nod of acquiescence from Mom, who was mopping up the spills from the stove-top and fighting back aggravated tears about to erupt from her eyes.

Jolinda launched into action and out the back door, retrieving her Blues Clues bicycle that had been leaning against the garage. She rode like the wind as she cycled down the street, feeling like this would surely earn her a special place in Mom's heart and most certainly (if there was any justice at all) it should earn her brother a giant grounding!

Jolinda was cautious at the corners, looking both ways and feeling just a little more grown-up. Arriving in a huff and slightly out of breath, she pounded on the door, and was greeted by Ron's mother, who was still on the phone! Opening the screen door with one hand and still talking into the phone resting between her shoulder and ear, she waved Jolinda in and pointed to a room.

As soon as Jolinda was about to yell at her brother and at Ron, she was halted by the sight of the two of them on the floor playing with the envy of her heart. Harsh words she'd carefully rehearsed all the way to Ron's house melted into a sweet cooing of: "Oh, what an adorable creature." Then, as if to catch herself missing out on the enjoyment of scolding her brother, she quickly added, "What are you doing playing with this silly creature when you are supposed to be home?!"

At that very moment, she realized the onslaught of a great opportunity! A magnificent plan was bubbling up inside her that could just well be what she was waiting for. Jolinda caught a glimpse of an idea that could turn her brother's misdeed into one of a possible good deed for herself. At once, her insides and her spirit lit up with a glimmer of hope that she might have discovered a loophole that would enable her to get her own pet ferret! The potential of it was too good to resist, so good in fact, that it replaced her desire to "rag" on her little brother and all the way back home her mind raced with how she might present this to her mother.

Jolinda had been trying to convince Mom that a pet ferret was just the thing she needed, one just like little Ron had. She had fallen in love at second sight (at first sight she screamed, thinking it was a rat) when Ron and her brother let her hold Alginon, a furry little ferret fellow. He had crawled right up from her hands to nuzzle in her neck and give her little kisses, nudging her to play with him from the beginning. She never really minded going to get her brother at Ron's house, from then on, just for the chance to pet and play with Alginon.

Jolinda thought it would be wise to wait until the next day, or maybe even a few days later, if she could possibly withhold her enthusiastic optimism about presenting her plan. Mom had disagreed with the notion of having any kind of pet to care for, but especially NOT a ferret, she'd said, adding that ferrets were stinky and could be mean. Jolinda had done some research, though, so she had ammunition to use against these false notions her mom had.

Four nights after the heroic act of helping Mom in a time of need, the moment of opportunity seemed perfect as Jolinda was setting the silverware on the table for dinner, noting that mom was in a good mood.

"Mom, I did a research paper in school on you know what," Jolinda blurted out as she added the napkins under the forks, "I got on 'A' on my essay on ferrets!" Seeing Mom lift one eyebrow with that sidelong glance she could get worried Jolinda for just a second, then they both broke into laughter in perfect moment of mutual understanding and a glimpse into the psychology of the statement!

"Okay, squirt, I see where you are going with this. You win, you can have a ferret but you have to promise that I don't have to nag you even once to take full care of it. If it stinks up the house, out it goes," Mom declared. Jolinda eagerly agreed and shared her findings that if a ferret is bathed regularly, fed the right diet, and treated with love and gentleness, it won't smell and will make a great pet.

Everything just seemed to fall into place. The next day in school, one of Ron's friends had discovered that his ferret was having babies. This information found no delay in being relayed to Jolinda and she made certain to confirm that she would like to have one of the litter when ready. Jolinda saved her allowance and did as many extra chores as she could to earn some extra cash to pay for a cage, leash, and a book on how to take care of a pet ferret. She'd be prepared when her little ferret was ready to take home.

The magical day came when she got to pick out the one of the litter, and she named it "Twinkie" as it was kind of a beige/yellow with white mottled in—looked just like her favorite treat to eat.

Knowing she would have to spend time bonding with it and training it, Jolinda didn't think too much about the difficult time she had with Twinkie over the first week. It seemed Twinkie got nervous when Jolinda would try to take him from the cage—so much so, he would even nip at her and hide in the corner of his cage.

She was just about to give up on Twinkie when that night she had a dream that Twinkie couldn't hear was, in fact, deaf. Upon awakening, she rushed to Twinkie's cage and instead of talking to her pet, she made a few hand gestures in sign language that she'd learned in school. At breakfast, Jolinda told her mother about her dream and her attempt at signing for Twinkie, but added in disappointment that it made no difference; he still seemed squeamish and frightened of her. Mama gave her the assurance that she would have to give this some time and if Twinkie truly was deaf, it would still take patience to teach him in a calm manner he could understand.

Jolinda couldn't help wondering if the ferret just didn't like her, but she persisted with calm movements and signing before every move she made. Within several more days, Twinkie began to calm down and come toward her when she approached the cage instead of running the opposite way to hide in a corner or under the bedding material on the floor of its domain. In no time, Jolinda and Twinkie bonded, cuddled, and played together. In fact, Jolinda told us, Twinkie didn't take kindly to anyone else except her, and that made Twinkie even more special to her. Jolinda's mother told us that she was amazed at how much more self-confidence her daughter seemed to have once this magical bond occurred. Jolinda's dream discovery and insight into her pet's bad behavior, and the subsequent closeness they shared on a near exclusive level, gave her a belief in herself and in her dreams—literally and figuratively!

*T*he International Campaign to Ban Land Mines estimates that 100 million explosive mines have been laid worldwide. Some of these deadly devices are set in the ground and covered with earth, others are positioned above ground and are triggered by tripwires. Planted during times of war with the deliberate intention of blowing up enemy tanks, armored vehicles, and foot soldiers, in periods of peace the mines kill or maim innocent men, women, and children.

Detecting these terrible hidden devices of death and destruction is not a simple task. Personnel armed with metal detectors often discover that their instruments cannot differentiate between a mine or a bit of scrap iron. Specially trained dogs are likely to become bored with the task, and they, too, can make a misstep and be blown up along with their human trainers.

The civil war in Mozambique ended twelve years ago, but in 2003 alone more than 10,000 mines were unearthed by experts who cautiously probed the earth. In spite of the diligent and courageous efforts of the mine detectors, fourteen people were killed or injured by mine explosions.

In a May 18, 2004, article carried by the *New York Times* News Service, Michael Wines reported on the progress being made in a program to train Gambian giant rats to detect land mines. According to the article, Frank Weetjens, a Belgian who works for an Antwerp demining group named Apopo, has a squad of sixteen pouched rats that have been successfully trained to sniff out land mines. Weetjens is of the opinion that the rats are better at detecting mines than either dogs or metal detectors. Havard Bach, the most recognized expert on demining techniques for the Geneva International Center for Humanitarian Demining, agrees that it would be better to use rats than dogs.

At an average of three pounds, the rats are much lighter than dogs and are less likely to detonate a landmine accidentally. Dogs bond closely with their owners and try always to please. Sometimes this can result in a fatal misinterpretation of an owner's body language. On the other hand, the rats care nothing for human approval and work strictly for food, running single-mindedly to sniff out mines in order to obtain the reward of a handful of peanuts—and when they are especially productive, a banana.

Weetjens called the journalist's attention to Wanjiro, a two-year-old Gambian giant pouched rat, outfitted in a red harness and hitched to a ten-yard clothesline. Wanjiro had recently been rewarded with food by her trainer, Kassim Mgaza, for accomplishing successfully the task of locating a land mine in the training field. About thirty inches long with nearly a foot of that length her tail, Wanjiro had sniffed the area until she located the hidden mine, then she scratched the red clay with both forepaws to mark the spot for her trainers.

Weetjen and his crew of trainers stated emphatically that the rats possessed a highly sensitive nose with a sniffing power equal to the legendary nostrils of the bloodhound. In November 2003, teams of Gambian rats were dispatched along a Mozambique railway that had been heavily mined during that country's seventeen-year civil war. The rats found every one of twenty live mines in a previously unsurveyed area of land.

Although the African rats are considered quite savage in their natural environment, they thrive in captivity and become quite docile. The mine-sniffing rodents may become major players in the solution to the dangerous problem of eliminating the deadly land mines scattered around the world. And they work for peanuts—with an occasional banana.

*I*n a recent series of tests conducted in the United Kingdom during the summer of 2004, researchers found evidence that sheep, while perhaps appearing to humans to be ruminating mindlessly in the pasture, may actually be thinking about their mothers, long-absent flock mates, or the shepherds who tend them. A team of scientists put a number of sheep in a darkened barn and showed them photographs of the faces of certain members of the flock, as well as the faces of goats or other animals. While the test group of sheep was being shown these photographs, the scientists were monitoring various indicators of stress, such as heart rate and the levels of cortisol and adrenaline hormones.

Later, it was clearly determined that the test group exhibited fewer signs of agitation when they were shown familiar sheep and human faces. After a series of experiments, the scientists concluded that their test group of sheep could recognize and remember at least fifty faces of their fellows and ten or more familiar human faces.

The research demonstrating that sheep can have more on their minds than munching grass reminded us of the story that Spence Roder told us about his father's pet sheep, Blackie.

"I grew up on a sheep ranch in Wyoming," Spence began his account. "We didn't have thousands of sheep and thousands of acres of grazing land like the really big ranchers, but we did have hundreds of sheep on a modest-sized piece of real estate and the flocks managed to keep us busy year 'round."

Spence remembered that his father had made a pet out of a black sheep named, strangely enough, "Blackie."

"Dad took to this black sheep of the flock ever since it was born," Spence said. "He fed Blackie from a bottle when he was a tiny lamb, and he even rocked him to sleep on a rocking chair on the front porch. Blackie loved to rock in that chair—even when he was full-grown. Dad would see him amongst a cluster of the other sheep, and he would yell out, 'Hey, Blackie! Do you want to rock?' And that crazy sheep would come running up on the front porch and jump into that old rocking chair."

Spence's mother had often been startled when she had come out to sit on the porch in the rocking chair and peel potatoes or mend some clothes. "She would be about to sit down in the chair when she would discover Blackie snoring away peacefully," Spence said. "Mom would yell something about 'who did that ball of wool think he was, the governor of Wyoming or the King of England?' And Dad would laugh and scold her not to disturb 'the King' from his beauty sleep."

Spence remembered that his mother would get on his father's case about spoiling Blackie and letting him rock on the front porch. She would warn, "If anyone were to drive up and see that dumb old sheep sitting there, rocking as if he owned the place, she would think you had lost your marbles."

"Dad would just laugh," Spence said. "Sometimes he would tease Mom that Blackie had been his Uncle Mel in a past life. Because Dad had sometimes been disrespectful to Uncle Mel when he was still alive, the old man had come back as a sheep and expected to be looked after like a king."

Spence said that he learned early in his life as a sheepherder that the flocks would always follow the leader of their particular little community. When he was just a boy of seven or eight, his father was having difficulty in getting a portion of the larger flock to go to a new pasture. Stubborn, none of them seemed interested in expanding their roaming and munching parameters. Then his father managed to get one of the older rams to jump a stone fence and walk into the new grazing ground. Within a few minutes, all the other sheep, one by one, jumped over the fence and joined the ram.

"Just remember, Spence," his father told him, "sheep always do what their leader does. I suppose in a lot of ways, sheep are like most people, just following their leader and letting him make all the big decisions."

One afternoon when Spence was eleven, he saw the leader of the sub flock (of which Blackie was a member) suddenly freeze in his tracks and bleat with fear. The sheep following closely behind the ram stopped, too, piling up on top of each other.

It didn't take Spence long to see the reason for the sudden traffic jam. In the middle of the path in front of the leader was a coiled rattlesnake, ready to strike.

"The sound of those rapidly vibrating rattles always sent a chill up my spine," Spence said. "Horses, cattle, and sheep know what that sound means. It means deadly fangs striking flesh and an almost certain death."

Spence was puzzled when the leader continued to stand, frozen, in front of the rattlesnake.

"The ram seemed too frightened to move," Spence recalled. "He seemed mesmerized by the snake and the ugly music it was making with its rattle. If Dad had been there, he would have shot the snake, but he was too far away to hear my shouts for help and to get there before the snake bit the lead ram. I thought about taking a chance and throwing a rock at the snake, but that would have only made him strike angrily all the faster."

Blackie was bleating in confusion along with the other sheep piled up behind their leader. Spence saw Blackie hanging back in fear—and then he got an idea.

"I knew one thing that would cut through Blackie's horror at seeing a rattlesnake," Spence said. "I yelled at the top of my voice, 'Hey, Blackie! Want to rock? Where's your rocking chair?'"

As if Spence were Pavlov ringing the bell for his conditioned dogs, Blackie immediately broke out of the deadly, spellbinding enchantment of the coiled rattlesnake and began to run toward the front porch of the ranch house, well over 100 yards away. The very instant that Blackie turned to trot off to the ranch house, the other sheep turned, too. Even the leader of the flock turned and followed Blackie.

"I know it was only my imagination," Spence said, "but the rattlesnake seemed kind of disappointed that it hadn't been able to strike one of the sheep. It slowly uncoiled and slithered off in the dust of the trail."

Now that the sheep were safely out of harm's way, Spence yelled for his father, who came on the run and shot the rattlesnake.

"Dad praised me for using my head and using Blackie's love for the rocking chair as a means of transforming him into the new leader of the flock," Spence said. His father wanted to find Blackie and give him a reward of a handful of salt.

"I'm sure he won't be hard to find," Spence said, gesturing toward the front porch off in the distance.

When they got to the front porch, they found Blackie rocking away contentedly while the thirty or so sheep that had followed him nibbled at bits of plant growth or stood placidly, as if awaiting further directions from their leader.

"If only we had a lot more rocking chairs," Spence laughed in recollection, "all those sheep would have been rocking away on the front porch."

$\mathcal{I}$n the spring of 2004, scientists at the Zoological Society of London were looking for volunteers to learn to "talk" chimpanzee. It was their contention that if humans behaved more like their chimp relatives, they would become more effective communicators.

Psychologist Cary Cooper is of the opinion that most people don't communicate their feelings as completely to their fellow humans as they should. Because chimpanzees are such close living relatives in genetic make-up as well as in expression and behavior, Professor Cooper suggests that humans might more easily resolve workplace conflicts, express emotions, and create strong bonds with others if we would "talk" more like the chimps.

For example, instead of talking about fearsome and demanding bosses behind their backs, office workers could show their fear by baring their teeth and using submissive body language, such as lowering their heads and crouching. Professor Cooper insists that while employees should not be aggressive toward those in authority, neither should they repress their feelings. Chimps and other animals, he maintains, are more tactile and supportive and comprise a strong community.

The experiments being conducted by the Zoological Society of London at their new chimpanzee facility at Whipsnade Wild Animal Park are devised to create better communications between chimps and humans so that it may be determined how to improve communications between humans and humans. As we conduct our ongoing research into the miracles that men and women have experienced with animals, we have encountered the stories of certain remarkable individuals who had already learned the secrets of animal and primate communication.

A few years ago, we heard about the powerful love bond that existed between filmmaker Richard Savage and Sunday, a white-breasted Capuchin monkey. The two of them lived for many years in a remote preserve in British Columbia where bears and wolves maintained their natural sovereignty over their wild kingdom. According to Richard, his little primate companion saved his life on more than one occasion.

Richard remembered the time that he was about to take out the garbage when Sunday began screeching and clutching at his hand. The whimpering sounds she was making caused the hair on the back of Richard's neck to stand up. Cautiously, Richard stepped outside, scanning his immediate surroundings for any sign of possible threat. He saw nothing.

Then, suddenly, a 700-pound grizzly bear lurched out of the trees and came lumbering toward him. Richard immediately understood that the bear wanted the tasty bag of garbage that he carried, so he dropped it and ran back inside the cabin.

Later, Richard said that he was certain Sunday's alarm had saved his life. If she hadn't warned him, Richard acknowledged, he could have been mauled to death. Yet, Richard explained, there was no way that Sunday could have seen the big grizzly from her vantage point inside the cabin. Sunday had a poor sense of smell, so it was unlikely that she caught the huge bear's scent. Richard doubted very much if she could have heard the bear. He simply could not understand how Sunday was able to know that violent death awaited him.

The next time that Sunday sounded her distress signal, Richard paid immediate attention. On this occasion, the devoted Capuchin kept running to the side of Savage's truck, making those same desperate whimpering sounds.

Savage got his rifle, once again anticipating the charge of a large predator. But what he eventually discovered could have been equally life-threatening. Richard got down on his hands and knees beside the area on the truck where Sunday kept making her pathetic whimpering sounds. He was startled to discover that he had ripped open a brake line on a rock and nearly all of the fluid had leaked out. If he had tried to drive down the mountain he lived on, he would have almost certainly crashed and possibly been killed.

When Richard was away on film assignments, he would leave Sunday with a writer friend. According to the friend who babysat Sunday, several minutes before Richard would call on the telephone to speak with him, Sunday would jump up and begin to chatter. After the call was completed, Sunday would sit down calmly. Sunday ignored the telephone for the entire day—until just before Richard called.

Sunday died a number of years ago, and Richard was left to grieve his beloved companion. But three nights after her death, he said, he awakened during the night and thought he felt the Capuchin's small, warm body snuggled against his shoulder in the familiar manner that Sunday had cuddled in life. Richard said that he knew then that his Sunday wasn't really gone. He was assured that their separation was only temporary parting.

Jan Randall of Sunnyside, Washington, is a loving woman, happiest when she is mothering somebody. Jan reared two children of her own, and then became a second mother to eleven kids when her sister became bedridden with a heart condition. Mothering thirteen children would be more than enough for most women—but not for Jan Randall, who has also taken in more than 200 foster children.

Mrs. Randall's only worry about mothering lies in the inevitable fact that all of her children will eventually grow up and leave her. She found the perfect solution to satisfy her emotional needs when she became the surrogate mother to Chee-Chee, a Manchurian macaque monkey.

In January 1992, Jan told reporters that the fully grown, thirty-seven-pound monkey was like Peter Pan, because at the mental age of a five-year-old human child, Chee-Chee will never leave her to strike out into the world on his own.

Jan acquired Chee-Chee as a newborn infant when a pregnant Manchurian macaque monkey was about to be sacrificed for medical research. Jan begged for the yet-unborn baby and was present to take the tiny thing into her hands at the moment of its birth. She fed the monkey from a doll's bottle filled with milk and water and treated the monkey as if she were a human baby.

Although Chee-Chee was given no particular household duties to perform, the Randalls stated that their "baby" once alerted the family to a smoldering fire in the attic just before the house burst into flames.

Gene, Jan's husband, went back into the inferno to carry Chee-Chee to safety, declaring to firemen that he had to rescue the monkey since she had saved their lives by sounding in alarm.

Although Jamie refers to her eight-year-old Capuchin monkey as her "baby," Jake is a talented housekeeper who has been trained to perform multiple duties for his mistress, who, as a quadriplegic cancer victim, is confined to a wheelchair.

Because of injuries received in an automobile accident when she was only sixteen years old, Jamie, thirty-four years of age, is able to move only her head and her shoulders, and her immediate world is mainly her apartment. A chin control that has been fitted to her wheelchair enables her to point at objects that she needs Jake to fetch for her. Unfortunately, if chin control mechanism moves even two inches to either side, it immobilizes Jamie's head. One of

Jake's most important jobs is to nudge the chin control back into place when it freezes Jamie's head movement.

At mealtimes, Jake scampers across the kitchen floor, opens the refrigerator door, and removes a large plastic container of prepared food. Nimbly, he carries the container in his tiny hands, returns to the table, and carefully spoon-feeds Jamie her meal. Should there be any leftovers, Jake returns the container to the refrigerator.

Helping Hands, the organization that trained the intelligent Capuchin to be such an efficient housekeeper, stated that Jake is even able to run a carpet sweeper to clean up the kitty litter mess that Jamie's two cats had spread across the floor.

Jake is not only a wonderful, loving pet, he is a set of helping hands that Jamie needs and relies upon on a daily basis!

andy Harrington of Charlotte, North Carolina, told us that she knows for certain that dogs go to Heaven because she witnessed her beloved dog's spirit being welcomed and received by an angel.

In March of 1990, Sandy purchased a Schnauzer pup and named him Zack. Sandy told us that Zack's personality was usually docile and quiet right up until the second her daughter, Joy, arrived home from school.

"At that moment," Sandy said, "he would jump down from my chair and charge into her heart. The shy dog vanished before our eyes and a dominant male force was born."

In time, Joy left home, and Sandy relocated to a nearby city where she married and later divorced. "Zack remained my constant companion," she said. "Each time I moved to a new neighborhood, Zack was obliged to explore his new surroundings. He'd sneak out of the house and disappear for days. About the time I was convinced he was hopelessly lost or dead, Zack would show up at the door with his head and tail hung low, ready and willing to accept his punishment. He'd bring various treasures to validate his adventure, including food, bones, and toys. Twice, he bore pellets from guns, which had to be surgically removed. Zack possessed the heart of a lion," Sandy continued. "He believed his duty was to protect me. When he was a puppy, Zack was crouching to attack two adult Doberman Pinchers. I caught him in the nick of time and managed to get him out of harm's way. We enjoyed good times and bad times. He always gave me unconditional love and inspiration. He was my rock!"

On a number of occasions, Sandy recalled that Zack actually became a real-life hero.

"He saved my husband, Wade, twice," Sandy said, "and he spared Joy from a panic attack. The first incident took place when Wade poured grease into a frying pan, turned on the gas burner, and left the kitchen to take a nap. As smoke filled the house, Zack jumped on

Wade's chest and barked frantically to wake him. Wade was able to put out the fire and no harm was done.

"The second time occurred when Wade had his fishing boat in tow. Zack began barking incessantly, making it impossible for Wade to focus on his driving. Angry, Wade pulled into a service station. Immediately, he spotted smoke bellowing from the rear of the boat. He found his jumper cable attached to the battery, sparking flames. If he hadn't stopped, the boat probably would have exploded en route."

Sandy explained that Zack's third act of valor was more chivalrous than heroic: "He caught a mouse in Joy's apartment. This deed greatly impressed her!"

After her divorce from Wade, Sandy and Joy moved into a new house that was furnished with all the modern conveniences, including a privacy fence encompassing the backyard. Zack was no longer required to act as protector. It was his time to relax and enjoy his golden years. But as fate would have it, his serenity was short lived.

In June of 2000, Zack began exhibiting signs of physical distress. Sandy said that he coughed continually and groaned throughout the night. "One evening, after I got home from work," Sandy remembered, "Zack couldn't seem to catch his breath. Joy and I rushed him to an emergency vet's clinic. After a brief examination, the vet informed us that Zack suffered from a heart arrhythmia. Taking pain and age into consideration, the vet recommended we put Zack down."

Sandy and Joy were shocked and devastated by the veterinarian's prognosis of Zack's condition. "We insisted on taking our beloved pet back to our car to determine his fate in privacy," Sandy said.

Although Joy wanted to return home with Zack, Sandy saw a look in Zack's eyes that told her he was tired, sick, and ready to die.

"I fought back my tears and begged God for the strength to do what I needed to do," Sandy said. "Joy and I caressed him, taking turns saying goodbye. At last, we got out of the car and carried Zack back inside the building."

The veterinarian explained the procedure to Sandy and Joy, saying that the first portion of the serum would relax Zack and the final dose would stop his heart. He warned them that fluids might excrete from Zack's body, making it even more difficult to endure. While the veterinarian was still detailing the process of putting Zack to sleep, Joy became physically ill. Tears flooded her eyes, and she ran out of the room.

As the vet squirted the excess fluid from the needle, Sandy clutched Zack and held him close. As quickly as the serum entered his blood stream, Zack's body relaxed and he fell back on the table. Almost immediately as the second dose was injected, Zack's heart stopped. His eyes glazed over and stared into space.

It was at that moment of parting that Sandy was blessed to behold a vision of farewell that she shall never forget.

"Time must have stood still at that precise instant!" Sandy told us. "I saw an orb of pulsating, golden light burst forth out of Zack's chest. This vibrant and quivering sphere sped past my chest, moving upward. Mesmerized, my eyes focused on the life force as it continued to move upward. Suddenly, Heaven opened up! The hand of an Angel was exposed, beckoning Zack's spirit to join her. Without pausing or looking back, Zack's spirit entered the light. Heaven's gate closed behind him. The vision disappeared.

"While I was watching this miraculous scene," Sandy continued with her marvelous account, "my emotions reacted accordingly. My psyche was jubilant, rejoicing at Zack's fate. Feelings of great rapture overcame my grief! Oblivious to what I was witnessing, the vet retained his sober demeanor. Thank God, I had the presence of mind to stop myself from laughing out loud. Such an outburst would've convinced the vet I was either insane or sadistic."

Sandy recalled that when the abstract reality that she had witnessed returned to normal, she stood speechless with her right hand resting on Zack's head.

"I didn't know whether to laugh or cry," she admitted. "So I walked out of the room, smiling. Joy saw my expression and thought Zack had been spared. Before she could question me, I ushered her outside. Then, I described what I had witnessed and my momentary jubilation. Joy didn't know how to react. But my conviction that I had witnessed Zack's ascension gave her solace, and she was comforted by the assurance that good dogs go to Heaven."

Four years have passed since Zack's death. Each time Sandy Harrington relives the extraordinary experience, she is overcome with emotion.

"For me, the scene is as vivid today as it was then," she told us. "I actually saw my beloved dog go to Heaven! Perhaps I cannot prove to everyone that this was so, but nothing will ever convince me that I didn't see an angel take Zack home.

"It's a mixed blessing to behold a miracle," Sandy said. "There's no way to describe it. There are simply no words to capture the beauty and energy of an ascending soul. The best adjective I can offer is 'awesome.'

"This is my story," Sandy told us, concluding her moving testimony to a beloved pet's survival after physical death. "I've presented it exactly as it occurred. You can accept it as true or false, according to your personal beliefs. But, as God is my witness, I'm reporting the truth."

*I*n 1990 when Iowa farmer Bill Davis accidentally ran over Rusty, his Australian red heeler, with a mower, he was horrified to see that he had pretty well mangled the dog's left legs.

The veterinarian had no choice other than to amputate Rusty's back leg below the knee and to leave little more than a stub of the front leg.

Just three days later, the tough pooch was walking on his two good right legs. In another six weeks, he was able to jump into Bill's pickup just like he did before the accident.

Things settled back to normal on the Iowa farm as Rusty herded the cattle with a kind of rabbit-like hopping run on his two right legs. Then, in 1993, someone struck the Australian red with a pickup truck, breaking his front shoulder and crushing his good back leg.

But Rusty was still game. By no means had he lost the will to live and to work. The veterinarian put four pins in the injured back leg, leaving the dog with only one good leg to hobble on.

Bill Davis marveled at how Rusty maintained such sweet disposition and great spirit. Never even for a brief time did the dog turn mean or bitter.

Early in 1994, when the vet removed the pins from Rusty's crushed back leg, the indomitable dog was immediately back to his determined self, earnestly herding cattle again on Bill's farm.

In 2001, Meg, a border collie on a New Zealand farm, was struck by a car and had to have her front left leg amputated. The feisty dog recovered from that accident, but six months later, she had a brutal collision with a four-wheel farm bike.

In this second accident, Meg suffered a crushed ankle and her right rear leg was split open. The tough border collie underwent two surgeries in an effort to save the leg, but it had to be amputated in October 2003.

While other sheep farmers would say that they had made every reasonable effort to save the dog and that it was now time to put her to sleep and save her from any further suffering, Meg's owner, Ian McDonald didn't see it that way. To him, Meg has been well worth the several thousand dollars that he has spent in veterinarian's bills.

Of course, Meg cannot defy gravity. With only two legs—a right front and a left rear—she falls down the moment she stops running around the flock. Gamely, though, she gets back up and moves quickly, efficiently doing her job. According to McDonald, Meg is still strong-willed and able to do her job with the sheep. She responds to all his instructions and his whistles and stills moves with ease around the flock.

*I*n July 2004, while the Wimbledon tennis championships were being played out, reporter Graeme Whitfield of *The Journal* reported that one of the most avid fans of the sport was a young rooster named Hen-Man.

Hen-Man resides in the home of Sally and Bill Weston, a couple who have kept poultry at Elemore Grange Farm near Pittington, County Durham, United Kingdom, for twenty-five years. In February 2004, the Westons were concerned that only one egg from a batch of twenty-four had hatched, so they kept the little fellow in their home to look after him.

After weeks of intensive care, the chick survived and became stronger but he continued to reside in the house with the Westons. He would follow Sally around the house as she did her chores and seemed more content in the house than outside with the rest of the chickens. After several weeks, the Westons realized that the chick, an Appenzeller-Spitshauben cross, had become too domesticated to be able to cope with the other chickens.

When the Wimbledon championships began, Sally was surprised when the rooster jumped up beside her on the sofa and appeared to be watching every move of the televised tennis match.

Sally found it difficult to believe, but the chick moved his head from side to side to follow the play. He seemed particularly excited when Tim Henman was on the court, so Sally and Bill decided that his little feathered admirer should be named after the tennis star.

Hen-Man truly seemed devoted to tennis in general and Tim Henman in particular. Once, when his hero lost in the quarterfinal, Hen-Man angrily shook his feathers, jumped off the armchair, and strutted away from the television set.

In other matches, Hen-Man sat transfixed by the court action. According to the Westons, he watched the ball going over the net, moved his head from side to side, and wouldn't budge from his perch on the armchair or sofa until all the players had left the court. Whenever Sally cheered in appreciation of a good serve, Hen-Man also squawked his approval.

The Westons admitted that Hen-Man did seem to like to watch television in general, but they held fast to their contention that tennis was his particular favorite and riveted his attention the firmest. Sally Weston theorized that what Hen-Man truly enjoyed the most about tennis was the cheering—and the squawking.

*K*irsten Moeller told us that she had named the large black-and-white cat Sophia because when she had first looked into the cat's gray-green eyes Kirsten felt that she could sense both wisdom and an indomitable spirit.

"Sophia just came to us, as did so many cats and stray dogs," Kirsten said. "My husband Andy and I live on an acreage near a fairly good-sized city in Illinois, and people are always dumping off their cats in the country when they tire of them. The rationalization seems to be that farmers always need more cats and farmers have plenty of milk and other food to feed an unlimited number of cats. That is simply not the case for the Moellers, but we feed the poor abandoned creatures anyway."

Kirsten and Andy are not farmers, but potters, and they make their living selling their handcrafted creations at craft shows throughout the Midwest and Southeast. In 1998, when their two daughters were married and living with their respective husbands in Chicago and Milwaukee, Kirsten and Andy decided that they would take a chance and do what they had always wanted. Andy left his job as a bookkeeper with a travel agency and Kirsten retired as a schoolteacher. They withdrew their savings to buy some land with an old farmhouse and a weathered but stable barn that was easily converted into a pottery studio.

Kirsten wouldn't begin to guess Sophia's breed or feline lineage. "To me she was just the very essence of 'cat'," she said. "Sometimes the disowned and abandoned cats would stay with us for a few days, sometimes for a few months. Then, as if they had some agenda to follow, they would decide it was time to move on. Sophia was quite obviously about to have kittens when she came to the acreage, and she definitely wanted to board with us for an indeterminate period of time."

Kirsten said that they had been living on the acreage for about two years before Sophia's unquenchable maternal instinct again came into play.

"In late spring, Sophia had five little black-and-white kittens in a crawl space that she had made under the tool shed," Kirsten said. "It was obvious that Sophia's entire existence was wrapped up in those kittens. She was always licking them, grooming them, feeding them with her milk. Andy and I saw her carrying them one by one by the nape of the neck to more spacious accommodations in one of the empty stalls in the barn. But a few weeks after they were born, some predator snatched them while Sophia was off catching mice for their breakfast."

Kirsten and Andy heard Sophia's plaintive cries as she searched for her babies. Neither of the Moellers knew what had taken the kittens away. They had been busy at their kilns turning out new pots to be sold at an upcoming craft show. The suspects included a feral cat, a raccoon, and the neighbors' huge and vicious German shepherd.

Sophia left the barn, Kirsten remembered, not aimlessly wandering in grief, but purposely, as if she knew the solution to her anguish.

Kirsten said that she watched with tears of her own as the desperate mother cat approached half a dozen baby chicks dozing in the late April sun.

"It was apparent that she was after new babies to replace the ones that something had stolen from her," Kirsten said.

The mother hen had other ideas. She charged at Sophia in such a rage that the cat cowered back against the chicken feeder. When the big rooster joined the hen, Sophia retreated under the barn.

Sophia disappeared for several days. Kirsten thought that she had moved on, sorrowing for her kittens, but Andy said that he had caught a couple of glimpses of her and thought that she was up in the hayloft.

About two weeks later, on a warm May afternoon while they were working in their studio, Kirsten and Andy beheld Sophia in all her maternal glory coming toward them from the corner of the barn nearest the hayloft ladder. Walking closely behind her were four black-and-white "kittens" with long fluffy tails.

"Andy!" Kirsten cried out in alarm. "Sophia has adopted four baby skunks!"

Andy told her not to be afraid. "Skunks won't hurt you unless you frighten them and they feel threatened," he said. "If Sophia wants babies so much, we might as well let her keep them. They kill a lot of mice and other vermin."

"But about their famous stink bombs?" Kirsten wanted to know.

Andy laughed at her understandable concern. "As long as we don't scare them or startle them, they won't shoot us. We're going to be so busy working on the new pots for the craft show next month that we won't even notice them. Besides, Sophia is taking care of them."

Kirsten said that Andy was absolutely correct. When it became apparent that Sophia was running low on her natural milk supply, the Moellers helped her out by putting out bowls of warm milk with bits of bread in them.

Later, Kirsten created a scenario of how Sophia had come to adopt her unusual kittens:

When the rooster and hen had chased her away from the chicks near the barn, Sophia had run into the woods. Here she found the orphaned skunks, mewing and hungry for food. Perhaps their mother had been shot by a hunter or killed by a predator. Sophia allowed them to nestle close to her body and drink her warm milk. They were even colored black and white, just as her real babies had been.

But before they could eat their fill, she pushed them away. She had to find them a new home where they would be safe. She picked the smallest one up by the loose skin at the back of its neck. She did not rest until she had carried all five of her new babies up to the farthest corner of the hayloft. She made a soft bed for them in the hay, gave them some more milk, then licked them and groomed them thoroughly with her rough pink tongue. The baby skunks felt at peace with their new mother, and Sophia purred and slept in contentment.

Every day Sophia's adopted babies grew bigger and stronger. Their eyes opened, and they saw for the first time the loving mother who cared for them so very much. Sophia brought them mice to eat, for the old hayloft was full of them. It wasn't long before the little skunks were catching mice on their own.

At last it was time to display her beautiful babies to Kirsten and Andy, who were working in their studio on the floor below. Once again, one by one, Sophia went down the hayloft ladder with a baby in her mouth. When she had them all safe on the ground floor, she started off for the studio, her babies walking behind her in single file.

"It wasn't long before the baby skunks were rubbing up against our legs just as they saw their 'mother' Sophia do," Kirsten said. "At first I was nervous and held my breath when a little skunk would rub up against my ankle as I was shaping pottery on the wheel, but after a few times, I would just reach down and pet it the same way that I did Sophia. And sometimes when my hand reached down toward them, they would lick me affectionately."

Humans cannot resist naming their pets, so after a few days Kirsten and Andy were calling the four skunks Donald, Huey, Dewey, and Louie. "We didn't know what genders they were," Kirsten admitted, "but they looked so cute following Sophia across the barnyard, always walking single file behind her."

The Moellers never had an unfortunate incident or accident with Sophia's adopted children. Even when customers drove up to claim a special order that Andy and Kirsten had crafted for them, the skunks were on their best behavior.

"Sometimes someone would ask if we had de-scented the skunks, and we would just kind of mumble an answer that they could interpret as reassurance that they weren't going to get sprayed," Kirsten said. "Other customers would drive away saying that they had heard that skunks could make good pets."

As it must occur to every mother sometime in her relationship with her children, Sophia's four babies left, one by one, to return to their natural habitat of the woods.

"By September, when they were about six months old, I guess the call of the wild had to be answered," Kirsten said. "Sophia seemed to sense that she couldn't fight natural instincts and she seemed to be resolved to losing her kids. One of the skunks stayed around a few days longer than the others, but one morning we noticed that he, too, had joined his kind in the woods."

Kirsten remembered how Sophia had jumped up on the worktable in the studio so that she could look into her eyes. "Some people may think it sounds silly," Kirsten said, "but I really feel that Sophia and I created some kind of mind link at that time. I really seemed to feel her pain and her sense of loss. In my mind, I told her, 'I know, Sweetie, it hurts us moms when our babies leave us, but such is the way of nature. Life goes on, and we just keep right on loving our babies whether they be near to us or faraway.'"

Sophia licked Kirsten's hand and purred, as if agreeing that only a mother could know the pain and the joy of having raised babies that could now go out into the world.

"I said aloud, 'Dear God, always keep our babies safe from harm and hurt,'" Kirsten said, concluding her story, "and I swear that Sophia nodded an 'amen.'"

*I*n a faraway galaxy known as the University of Michigan Medical School, in a place known as the Geriatrics Center, Yoda lives in happy contentment with Princess Leia.

No, not that Yoda, the pointy-eared, Hobbit-like, instructor of Jedi knights. Nor that Princess Leia, the feisty warrior queen with the strange hairdo. The happy couple we're talking about have bodies covered with hair, rather large, rounded ears, and twitchy, whiskered noses.

On April 10, 2004, this particular Yoda became the world's oldest known dwarf mouse when he celebrated his fourth birthday. At 1,462 days old, Yoda is now the equivalent age of about 136 human years.

The lifespan of the average laboratory mouse is just a bit over two years. Yoda is only the second mouse the scientists at the medical school know to have made it to his fourth birthday.

And who is Princess Leia? According to the scientists at the lab, dwarf mice are always housed with larger females to provide the males with body warmth so they won't freeze to death.

$\mathcal{I}$t was nearly the final checkered flag for Pierre the racing pigeon when he crashed into the grille of George and Irene Cowrie's Citroen C5 while they were on vacation in France. Neither George nor Irene noticed the collision when it took place, and they returned to England none the wiser that they had a feathered citizen of Calais hitchhiking along with them, albeit against his will.

Two days after they returned to their home in Warwickshire, George thought that he saw a feather sticking out of their automobile's grille. He bent down to pull it out—and discovered that there was a pigeon attached to the feather.

Unable to pull the bird free and not wishing to injure it any further, George took the car to a local garage owned by Robin Coldicott. Fortunately, Robin's wife Sue was a former veterinary nurse who very ably and gently removed the pigeon from its uncomfortable temporary roost.

Pierre had suffered a broken leg and a damaged wing when he smashed into the grille of the Citroen C5, but he appeared to be none the worse for wear from his ordeal. An identity tag on his leg provided the details of the racing pigeon's place of origin in Calais, and the Coldicotts cared for Pierre until he could be reunited with his owner.

In the autumn of 2004, a lovely and personable goat named Lucy won first place in a beauty contest for goats that was held in the village of St. Vincenat in western Croatia. Ivan Perko, Lucy's owner, said that he was not surprised. He had always thought that Lucy was the most beautiful goat in his village of Most Rasa, and now the decision of the judges had proved it by naming her the most beautiful goat in the world. There was no prize for being crowned first place, but Perko said that the singular honor would be enough for Lucy and him.

Organizers of the beauty contest explained that they had come up with the idea as a means of drawing attention to the grim fact that traditional goat farming is dying out in Croatia. At one time there were 800,000 goats in the Istria region, but today there are only about 1,000.

Although it is difficult to arrive at precise numbers of the goat population in the United States, experts estimate that on the nation's farms and ranches there are between two to three million representatives of one of the oldest domesticated animals in the world. While goat milk is not terribly popular in the United States, more goats' milk is consumed worldwide than cows' milk.

Our friend Cliff says that he never gets tired of hearing his Uncle Sam Torkelson tell about his pet goat Gus and the time they ended up in a parade. Not long ago, we were privileged to hear the story for ourselves.

Sam grew up in a small farming community in southern Minnesota and, as he tells it, he "inherited" Gus when his friend Sandy and his folks moved off the farm.

It was 1943, Sam remembered, and Sandy's father, Martin Palmer, decided to move into the city to work at a defense plant. The Palmers had been struggling to make ends meet on the family farm since the Depression left them nearly broke, so Martin was saying goodbye to the good earth of the farm and saying hello to the concrete canyons of the city. Sixteen-year-old Sandy said that there was no way he could take his goat Gus with him, so, choking back tears, he bequeathed the goat to Sam.

Sam was particularly excited to inherit Gus because Sandy had trained him to pull a cart, and the bright red cart came with the goat.

"Just remember, Sam," Sandy warned him. "Gus is a country goat, born and bred. He's no city goat. He's afraid of loud noises and noisy people. He gets really jumpy if he hears any bang or boom. He'll take off running for his stall in the barn and he won't stop until he gets there and feels that he's good and safe."

Sam knew that Sandy had issued that warning because Sam's family farm was only a mile from town. "He didn't have to be a prophet to foresee me wanting to drive Gus into town and show off for the town kids. I was eleven years old, I wasn't about to hide my light—or my goat—under a bushel basket."

Sam explained with echoes of childlike pride that Gus was an Anglo-Nubian goat. The breed had been brought to the United States from England in the early 1900s and was developed by crossing British milk goats with goats of African and Indian origin.

"The Anglo-Nubian goat is one of the heaviest and tallest of all the breeds of goat," Sam said, "and the bucks, the males, get really big. I would guess that old Gus probably weighed over 150 pounds, so I was glad that Sandy had done the training and conditioning him to pull a cart."

Gus had a rather large head with a roman nose and long, wide, pendulous ears that hung close to his cheeks. His short hair was reddish-colored with white patches.

"Every day, I would hitch Gus to the red cart, climb in, slap the reins, and yell, 'Giddyap!'" Sam said, smiling at the memory. "Old Gus would step out proudly, tossing his head in the air so his long ears would flap around his head. He really seemed to like pulling the red cart with the happy kid inside."

One day, Sam's mom needed some chicken feed, and he heard her complaining that she didn't have time to drive into town and pick some up. Sam volunteered his and Gus's services to travel the mile into town to get it.

"Mom told me to be careful and be mindful of any cars coming or going on the gravel road," Sam said, "but I could tell she was grateful not to have to take the time to drive into town."

Sam and Gus pulled up beside the loading dock at Carlson's Feed Store, and Billy O'Hern put the feed in the back of the cart. He packed it in with newspapers so it wouldn't spill if the coarse burlap sacks split on the bumpy ride home.

Sam started home, but when he reached the corner of the street he saw Constable Brandon directing traffic. Sam was confused because there usually wasn't much traffic to direct in their small town. There had to be something unusual going on in the community that day. Constable Brandon shouted at Sam to turn left, so he did as he was told.

At the next corner, Mr. Westerberg, the town marshal, was also directing traffic. He told Sam to turn his cart to the right. By that time, Sam noticed small groups of people beginning to line the main street.

"Marshal Westerberg got impatient and yelled at me again to turn right, so I pulled on the reins and headed Gus toward the right," Sam said. "That's when I heard the first blast of the trumpets from the high school marching band. I realized that there was some kind of parade and goings-on in town—and that I had better high-tail it for home before Gus got scared and started to run."

Sam was just feeling grateful to Marshal Westerberg for directing him away from the noisy parade route when old man Bratrud, who owned one of the grocery stores in town, ran right up to the cart and shouted at Sam to turn to left.

"Hurry, Sam, hurry up with that goat!" Mr. Bratrud commanded. "Turn left!"

The memory of previous negative experiences with Mr. Bratrud reminded Sam that there was no arguing with the man.

"So I turned left," Sam said, laughing at the recollection. "And I turned smack dab into the parade itself."

Around the corner came the marching band, trumpets, trombones, and bass horns blaring, kettledrums rattling, clarinets and saxophones wailing. And rows and rows of boys and girls pulling wagons filled with newspapers, magazines, and scrap metal behind their bicycles. There were kids with pony carts and dogcarts, too. Some girls pushed baby buggies and doll buggies, all of them stacked with discarded paper products. Six boys marched in front of the band carrying banners that read:

Bring Your Old Papers and Scrap Metal to the School. Support the War Effort. Remember Our Boys Fighting for Our Freedoms.

"I realized then that there was a scrap paper and metal drive in town that day," Sam said. "The men directing traffic had seen the papers in the back of my cart and thought that I had come into town to be in the parade."

At the very moment of Sam's realization of the fix that he was in, the brass section thundered loudly and the crowd lining the streets let out a mighty cheer.

"That was too much for Gus," Sam said. "He took off as if he had heard Gabriel's trumpet in that marching band coming toward us. I tried to pull on the reins and slow him down, but there was no stopping him. We tore off straight through the parade, scattering members of the marching band every which way. Gus didn't slow down for the boys and girls on their bikes pulling wagons or the ponies pulling carts. We sent them all running for safety."

Sam had no control over Gus and absolutely no influence on his decision-making processes. He did all he could do to hang on to the jolting, bouncing, swaying cart.

Ahead of them, Sam could see a group of men and women standing in front of the high school. As Gus ran toward them, one of the men raised his arms and shouted that they were supposed to stop and leave their paper and scrap metal there.

"Stop!" the man yelled. "Put the paper in that pile. The scrap metal on the flat bed of the truck! Stop!"

Sam shouted back that he couldn't stop. He was in a runaway cart. Desperate to return to his stall, Gus headed back toward the parade and what he knew was the right direction to run home.

"I could see that some of the men were laughing at me—the dumb kid who couldn't control his goat," Sam said. "I was so shaken up and scared that I almost started to cry. But then, I knew, the men would really laugh at me."

The group of men who were laughing the loudest at Sam's misfortune saw that Gus had suddenly turned and was heading straight toward them.

"I remember that crowd of men opening up just like Moses parting the Red Sea," Sam said, "and Gus ran straight through them."

Now Gus seemed to be confident that he was heading back to the farm. He kept on running until he was out of town and out of breath, and then he had to slow down.

"But he kept up a kind of trot until he was safe and sound in his own stall in the barn," Sam said.

Sam's mother asked what had taken them so long. "You didn't stop at the drugstore to look at any comic books, did you?"

Concluding his story with a warm chuckle, Sam said that he told his mother that he had just survived an adventure far crazier than any he had ever read in a comic book.

"Of course it didn't take long for Mom and Dad to hear the full story of my misadventures in town," Sam said. "Most of the reports they heard were extremely exaggerated. Fortunately, no one had been hurt by Gus's wild charge, but I was teased for years about the way I had enlivened the parade. Neither Mom nor Dad had to order me to not bring Gus and the cart to town again. Sandy had meant it when he warned me that Gus was definitely a country and not a town goat, and I never even thought about driving him to town again."

*T*s your dog a "Bowser" or a "Prince"—or do you confuse people in the park when you throw a Frisbee and call out for "Jim" or "Sarah" to catch it in their teeth?

Do you recite phrases over and over so that "Pretty Bird," the parakeet, will repeat them, or do you talk to "Melvin" as he contentedly pecks at seeds in his cage?

Is it "Fluffy" that you summon up on your lap to pet, or do you coax "Loretta" into eating her cat food?

In 2004, Pastor Reinaldo from Rio Grande do Sul, Brazil, began campaigning for a new law that would ban people in his South American country from giving human names to pets. In his opinion, it is terribly embarrassing for people to find out that they have the same name as a dog, cat, or goldfish. Under his proposed new law, anyone who gives animals a human name would be fined and ordered to carry out community service.

We hope such a law is never passed in the United States, for we would quickly be found guilty of violating the rules with our predilection for christening our pets with such names as Fred, Leonard, Moses, Bart, and Carlotta. Surely, we have had a "Queen" or a "Pretty Girl" or "PussKat" in our time, but we do consider our pets members of the family—and because we prize their individuality, it seems to us appropriate to bestow a fitting human name upon them.

While many individuals have taken that same warmly intended appellation "member of the family" to heart, there is no question that some men and women have applied it a greater extent than others.

When twenty-eight-year-old dentist Liz Wales prepared for her nuptials with Geoffrey Glass, she made no bones about the fact that Sooky, her beloved dog, would be an integral part of her nuptials. On her wedding day in Glasgow, Scotland, Ms. Wales made her three-year-old dog a member of her wedding party. The pooch was, in fact, one of the four bridesmaids.

Well aware of his bride's genuine case of puppy love for her mixed-breed canine, Glass wisely raised no objections to the inclusion of Ms. Sooky in the wedding party. Sooky was even the guest of honor during the reception and was seated in a special place at the bridal table.

The bride declared to her wedding party that Sooky was one of the family. Since this was her special day, the new Mrs. Glass said, she definitely wanted Sooky to be part of it.

For their August wedding, Mike Knecht and Tracy Hill of Red Deer, Alberta, Canada, asked Mike's dog Bandit to serve as the best man. All those in attendance agreed that Bandit was on his very best behavior and admirably performed all the duties of best man and best friend.

At the outdoor wedding of Kimberly and Paul in Hamilton, New Jersey, two of the flower girls and the ring bearer were dogs. Kimberly, a dog groomer, proudly explained that the whippets were like her children.

Duke, the ring bearer, was outfitted in a gray doggie tuxedo with a pink ruffle on his shirt. The flower girls, Cameo and Knee-Hi, wore white lace gowns.

The three special members of the wedding party were all show dogs, so they were accustomed to being on their best behavior. Kimberly told reporters that there was no way that she could have left them home during this most important moment of her life.

Lee Day, dog groomer, staged the lavish ceremony for Tammy Faye Bakker's Yorkshire terrier Corky and a white poodle named Peaches. Each of the canines wore elegant formal wedding attire, and the ceremony was televised and witnessed by the enormous Praise the Lord network audience as the two dogs were united in Christian marriage.

In July 1993, Margaret McDowell and David Cooper honeymooned in the hotel where their dogs had brought them together just a few months earlier.

Both Margaret and David were on weeklong vacations with friends at a hotel in Devon, England, when David's dog Ike first got a good look at Margaret's dog Mara during a walk on the grounds.

The dogs' noses met, David chuckled later in retelling the story, and he and Margaret just happened to be on the other end of the leashes. Ike and Mara seemed to take an instant liking to one another, and so did David and Margaret.

After a brief conversation, the two vacationers went their separate ways and rejoined their friends, but David couldn't get Margaret's lovely Irish voice out of his mind. Margaret, of Belfast, Ireland, had likewise noted David's nice voice and the loving manner in which he treated his dog. Margaret and David have to rely upon such verbal impressions, for they are both blind.

When the two met again that night in the dining room, they began to talk in earnest and they learned that they had an extraordinary number of things in common. By the second night, they were holding hands. By the fourth night, David confessed that he had fallen in love and sincerely believed that they would end up married to one another.

Although smitten, Margaret felt that things were moving just a bit too fast for her. After a tearful farewell, the two, both telephone operators, were soon calling each other daily from work and once again at home in the evening. After a few more weeks, David was flying to Belfast from his home in Worthing, England, for weekend visits.

After a few more months of such long-distance romancing, the two decided to get married and to honeymoon at the Devon hotel where they had met. Their beloved dogs, Ike and Mara, served as their escorts with resounding barks of approval.

Commenting on how close the two dogs had become, David suggested that the dogs may have played Cupid as part of a very cunning plan—maybe Ike and Mara brought them together because they wanted to be together!

Newlyweds Josephine and Stewart chose to live forty miles apart, in separate houses, because they discovered after their marriage ceremony that their two female dogs hated each other. Both Josephine and Stewart raised their dogs from pups, and neither could bear to be separated from their pets.

The couple had married with the intention of living in Stewart's house, but then they discovered that Josephine's Labrador, Tanya, and Stewart's springer spaniel, Gale, seemed jealously determined to maul each other at every opportunity. Both Josephine and Stewart had suffered bites while trying to separate the two dogs; and one occasion, after a particularly vicious skirmish, Stewart had to be taken to the hospital.

The best the couple could come up with until one of the dogs died was to travel to each other's home three or four times a week. On those visits, Gale sleeps in Stewart's car and Tanya stays in Josephine's van.

One of the most bizarre custody cases on record in U.S. courtrooms took place on September 5, 1990, when Linda Walker of Novi, Michigan, won custody of her beloved pythons—fourteen-foot-long Samson and four-foot-long Jake. Ms. Walker told reporters that the pythons were her "babies," and she loved them just as much as any mother loved her children.

In July 1990, when Linda first divorced Terry, she won custody of both pythons. But after she moved out of their house, she asked her ex-husband if he would keep Samson, the big guy, until she could find new living quarters.

Terry accommodated her, and all seemed fine until sometime in August when Linda learned that Samson had nearly been run over by a car while Terry was taking him for a "walk." Outraged by the incident—which had even been reported in a local newspaper—Linda demanded that Terry return the fourteen-foot python immediately.

This time, however, Terry was not quite so accommodating. He argued that possession was nine-tenths of the law, and he refused to return Samson.

Fortunately for Linda's maternal concern for her "baby," the same county judge who had originally granted her full custody of her "children" once again decreed that she should received custody of both pythons.

Before Helen Walsh died in 1987 at the age of eighty, she made certain that her two canine companions, Nickie and Carla, would be able to remain in her Memphis, Tennessee, home until their natural deaths. In addition she saw to it that there would be ample finances set aside to provide food and veterinary care for as long as they lived.

In 1986, the eccentric Austrian countess Carlotta Liebenstein was visiting the Italian village of Fauglia when she spotted a German shepherd and developed an immediate fixation upon him. In her mind, she named him Gunther III in memory of earlier shepherds that she had owned, and when she heard him "singing" in his deep-throated howl, her fixation graduated to a full-blown obsession. She even bought a house in the village so that she could be near the handsome German shepherd. Eventually, she bought Gunther III from his original owners.

Before the countess's death, she was often heard to express her great disappointment that all people did not love dogs with the same passion that she expressed toward Gunther III. She ordered her will rewritten so that her vast estate would be left to the newly created Gunther Foundation Trust, an organization whose sole task would be to help educate humans to gain a more complete understanding of the vast reaches of canine love.

When Carlotta Liebenstein passed away in 1991, her entire fortune of $80 million was bequeathed to her beloved German shepherd. When Gunter III died a month later, the trust went to his heir, Gunther IV, thus making him the world's richest pet.

o one could fault Elena Flora for being startled when she answered her sheepdog Vasile's barking and scratching at the front door of her home in Raducaneni, Romania, and found him carrying a bundle, which she later found out contained a newborn baby.

Elena looked at her watch and saw that it was the middle of the night. It was unlike Vasile to roam far from home and not come home immediately when she called him. She must have fallen asleep on the sofa waiting up for his return.

At first, she admitted that she had become very frightened. Vasile was whining and pacing, and she was almost afraid to open the bloodstained bundle of cloth that he had dropped gently at her feet. And when she discovered what appeared to be a newborn baby boy wrapped in swaddling clothes, she feared that Vasile might have stolen the infant from someone's home. Knowing that she had to notify the authorities as soon as possbile, Elena called the mayor, and he, in turn, summoned the police and an ambulance.

With Vasile's assistance, investigating officers found the exact place in a field two miles from Elena Florea's home where the baby had been born and abandoned by his mother. Traces of blood and clothing remained at the spot where Vasile had gathered the infant's swaddling clothes in his jaws and carried the newly born child home to Elena.

Because of Vasile's prompt action in rescuing the abandoned baby, the ten-pound infant received proper care and attention at a hospital in Lasi.

A few years ago, we learned of the unique missionary work of Reverend Wendell Hansen, who was assisted by four macaws, four Amazon parrots, and two cockatiels in bringing inspirational messages to audiences throughout the United States. In addition to those ten feathered messengers of the Word, Reverend Hansen had a backup crew of twenty other birds to help him spread biblical teachings.

At that time, the eighty-three-years-young Indiana minister had taught his birds to talk, sing, ride miniature bicycles, climb ladders, and perform a wide variety of other actions—all of which were designed to deliver a message of inspiration and hope.

Assisted by his son Dean and his wife Eunice on piano and organ, Reverend Hansen brought his traveling gospel bird show to audiences in thirty states. A conventional minister in his younger years, Reverend Hansen developed the unusual concept of using birds to inspire men and women and bring them the power of messages from the Bible. He said that he began training the birds to speak "human talk" when they were just babies, before they learned to communicate with "bird talk."

As part of his religious program, Reverend Hansen would ask John, a yellow nape Amazon parrot, what he said when he went to church. Right on cue, John would squawk his earnest reply: "Praise the Lord!"

When he received a compliment from Reverend Hansen for having given the correct answer, John would sing out, "Hallelujah!"

Reverend Hansen said that he would never forget to give the birds a treat whenever they responded with the right words. And thus his faithful flock of thirty birds was created.

When Brian Bisler saw Ben, his sheepdog, carrying a bottle in his mouth, he knew that something was wrong. The stalwart Ben was not in the habit of picking up discarded bottles and bringing them into the farmyard.

Retrieving the bottle from the dog's mouth, Bisler, a farmer who lives outside of Falkirk, Scotland, saw a note in it. Perplexed, Bisler broke open the bottle and was startled to read a desperate plea for help from Robert Sinclair, a fellow everyone knew as a hermit who foraged off the land. Bisler was aware that Sinclair had been living in a deserted farmhouse not far from his own farm.

Sinclair's note said that he was in severe pain and was unable to move from the farmhouse. He had depleted his stores of food and water, and he feared that he would die alone in the old house.

Within minutes of reading this, Bisler summoned emergency services and help was on the way to the fifty-five-year-old hermit who had survived off the land for twenty-seven years or more. When the emergency personnel arrived at the farmhouse where Sinclair had been living, they found him gasping for breath. Quickly diagnosing a possible asthma attack, they administered oxygen and took him to the acute ward in the Falkirk Royal Infirmary.

Rescue workers later told Brian Bisler that the first words Sinclair managed to say after they had given him some oxygen was, "Thank you, Ben!"

Sinclair had been without food for eight days and without water for four when he saw the dog through his window. His last hope was to write the note, put it in a bottle and, mustering his last bit of strength, throw it out the window where he prayed the sheepdog would see it and bring it to his master. Bisler told the *Falkirk Daily Record* that he was proud of Ben. "If it wasn't for him," he said, "Robert would probably have died."

$\mathcal{I}$f you happened to look in John Spafford's backyard, it is not a quaint little dog house sporting a "Fido" sign that you see, but a pet of a far different nature and breed. The shock might cause you to look away at first, but then the intrigue would no doubt fasten your gaze to a fixed stare as your mind tried to rationalize how you could really be seeing the eighty-some lizards crawling around the yard! Yes, we said lizards!

John Spafford, a mechanic in Mandarin, Florida, would—according to locals—be more likely to have a yard full of broken-down old car engines and bodies awaiting his expert skills to repair, but lizards? It all started when John, who is a good father, wanted to give his beloved daughter a different sort of pet for a gift. It turned out both father and daughter loved the pet lizard, which was in fact a gecko, so much that it grew into a hobby. They decided to share the joy of pet lizard ownership with others and began breeding them; one thing led to another and voilà—an entire yard full of—lizards and dragons. The Spaffords have added still more breeds of lizards, and their menagerie now includes monitor lizards and bearded dragon lizards.

According to the July 7, 2003, issue of *The Jacksonville Business Journal*, Spafford is not unique. There is a tremendous surge in "exotic pet" enthusiasts who are really taking to the idea of owning out-of-the-ordinary pets, and many of these same enthusiastic individuals are also breeding the creatures.

Part of the amplified popularity of exotics pets might be due to an ever-increasing number of people who suffer from pet allergies, especially those who are allergic to dogs, cats, and birds. Lizards, especially, are increasingly being purchased and are gaining in numbers as a favorite family pet.

There are some 700 to 900 varieties of lizards, including one that is said to be the most sold reptile in North America: the green iguana.

Eleven-year-old Polly Rodriguez found it a dreaded fate to go to bed at night. Each evening she would dally and find umpteen more things to do, even homework, which she still preferred to shutting out the lights and calling it a day. Mrs. Rodriguez eventually won what had become the battle of bedtime using an innovative technique based on "animal psychology."

"Mom noticed how curious I was when I saw her reading a book she received as a gift; the book was *Animal Miracles*," Polly wrote in a letter to us. "When Mom told me she would read a story from your book if I got ready for bed and into bed, without the normal protest and dawdling I found myself hurrying to go to bed.

"It soon became routine, and before I knew it, I was actually looking forward to going to bed just so I could hear Mom read the next story from your book."

Then Polly went on to describe a most unusual pet that she talked her mom into getting for her birthday: a pet iguana! "I think Mom only allowed me to have it because things had been going so smoothly and she saw how much I wanted to have a pet," Polly confessed.

Polly's mom was highly allergic to animal dander, including cats, dogs, rabbits, birds, and so she agreed that Polly could have her very own pet iguana following a demonstration of iguana behavior and care given by Scott, a neighbor. Polly had become enamored of Yoshi, Scott's iguana pet, and with Scott's brilliant ploy of asking Mrs. Rodriguez if she would come see the new house he'd built for Yoshi, Mrs. Rodriguez would discover she wasn't sneezing when she walked into Scott's room, so that she wouldn't have an excuse.

"I learned all about how to care for iguanas first, then told my mom of my research and dedication," Polly said, adding, "I knew just the one I wanted at the pet store and he's been my buddy ever since! Iggy is the best thing that ever happened to me."

Polly wrote that she has a leash for Iggy and takes him everywhere with her.

"He's making a lot of friends for me, too," she added. "Wherever I take him, people crowd around me to see him and ask me questions about him. Guys think it's cool that a girl has a pet lizard. My green iguana named Iggy is beautiful and gentle, and I really love him. It turned out to be a good thing my mom was allergic to all the normal kinds of pets, so I could have Iggy!"

When we were lecturing in Hawaii, we were startled by a sudden, outrageous, unidentified creature sound. The first night there, while reading in our chairs and preparing for the day ahead, we heard the strangest, loudest "Brrrrrraaaaaaaaaap" we'd ever heard. Looking at each other with startled expressions and puzzling over where in the world that noise could have come from, our gaze was drawn directly over our heads to a tiny little green creature that again let out a bellow we thought would rival any dragon's. We came to find out it was a friendly gecko, sometimes allowed to wander into homes because they eat a variety of troublesome insects. We thought you might want to know about these loud belching noises before getting a pet gecko! Perhaps they could be trained to bellow out the "Star Spangled Banner" or something else on cue or to appear on David Letterman's "Stupid Pet Tricks."

Just kidding. But in all seriousness, please take the advice of many pet owners before purchasing an exotic pet, whether it is a gecko, lizard, or any other kind of animal. Do some research to learn about the pet to determine if it is really right for you and not just a novelty. All pets, from ants to dragon lizards, hermit crabs to tarantulas, deserve and require love, care, and the proper attention—as they are all part of God's wonderful, expansive world of MIRACLES!

A national poll conducted a few years ago revealed the somewhat shocking statistics that three out of four pet owners talk more to their pets than to their spouse, sweetheart, or significant other. When men and women who said that they were pet owners were asked if they talked to their pet than their partner, an astounding 73 percent answered yes. And there was almost no difference between the genders: 74 percent of men and 72 percent of women admitted that they more often preferred to talk things over with pooch, pussycat, or parakeet.

Although this is a book in which numerous cases of wonderful, inspirational, and miraculous interactions have been reported and we have freely admitted that we have always regarded our pets as family members, the authors do not advocate any of our readers excluding the company of humans when it comes to matters of confidence or emotional expression. Please remember that your pet needs to be recognized and respected as a loving member of a companion species and prized for its own unique contributions to your life. Our pets are not surrogate humans. They are sovereign entities in their own right, and they touch our hearts and our souls in their own special ways.

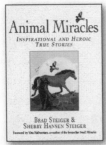